Everything and the Kitchen Sink

Everything and the Kitchen Sink

Remodel Your Kitchen Without Losing Your Mind

JANICE ANNE COSTA AND DAINA MANNING

Andrews McMeel
Publishing

Kansas City

05 06 07 08 09 10 WKT 10 9 8 7 6 5 4 3 2 1

Library of Congress Cataloging-in-Publication Data
Costa, Janice Anne.
    Everything and the kitchen sink : remodel your kitchen without losing your mind / Janice Anne Costa and Daina Manning.
        p. cm.
    Includes index.
    ISBN: 0-7407-5019-4
        1. Kitchens—Remodeling. I. Manning, Daina. II. Title.

TH4816.3.K58C67 2005
643'.4.4—dc22

2004057477

Book design by Holly Camerlinck

Attention: Schools and Businesses
Andrews McMeel books are available at quantity discounts with bulk purchase for educational, business, or sales promotional use. For information, please write to: Special Sales Department, Andrews McMeel Publishing, 4520 Main Street, Kansas City, Missouri 64111.

Front cover photos (clockwise, from top left):
Forbo
DuPont Zodiaq
Walker Zanger
CaesarStone
Bruce Zickuhr, AIA (Metropolitan Designs); Photo by Richard Sprengler

Back cover photos (left to right):
Gary White, CMKBD, CID (*Kitchen and Bath Design*); Photo by Larry Falke
Gary White, CMKBD, CID (*Kitchen and Bath Design*); Photo by Larry Falke
John Sofio (Built, Inc.); Photo courtesy of Lone Pine Pictures

To Jan's mom and dad, for a lifetime of love, faith, and support;
And to D's husband, Michael Manning Jr., best friend, partner in crime,
and overall best thing that ever happened to me.
We couldn't have done it without you.

CONTENTS

ACKNOWLEDGMENTS

A book is a collaborative effort. This book would never have been possible without the help of our many wonderful colleagues, supporters, and friends, especially:

Kitchen & Bath Design News publisher Eliot Sefrin, a brilliant writer, wonderful mentor, and dear friend, whose enormous knowledge of and passion for the kitchen design industry have been an essential resource to both of us.

The *K&BDN* editorial team, especially John Filippelli, Barbara Capella Loehr, and Anita Shaw, and our wonderful art director Laura Froehlich, whose assistance and support have been invaluable in making this project happen. Many thanks for your endless patience and willingness to take things off my desk so this could actually get done!

The *K&BDN* family—Chris Kirkby, Joanne Naylor, Kim Carroll, Rick Dahl, Nancy Campoli, Noble Laird, Traci Brooks, and Lynnell Lischka—a privilege to work with and a pleasure to know, as well as Kathy Scott and Ingrid Volkerts for their professional assistance.

Ellen Cheever, Mary Jo Peterson, Karla Krengel, John Morgan, Steve Nicholls, Sarah Reep, Ralph Palmer, Alan Asarnow, Linda Jennings, Lori Fradella, and all of the kitchen industry professionals whose talents continually inspire us. We would also like to thank all the designers and manufacturers who lent their support and beautiful photos to this book, particularly Jeff Clark, Gary White, John Sofio, and Fu-Tung Cheng for their stellar interpretations of modern design.

Jan's support network: Barbara and Charles Garnar, Kathleen and Philip Delakas, Gail Plotnick, Carol Lamb, Bob Dealy, Josephine O'Brien, Susan Harper, Marcia Boxenbaum, Frank Bonomo, Cyn Mobley, and the gang at Utopia, with deepest thanks for your friendship, support, and occasional talking me off the ledge.

D's wonderful in-laws, Sue Manning and the late Michael Manning Sr., and all of the Manning clan for their support, as well as the SoCal Film Group. And Foster, Coney, and Liberty, for being understanding all those times they got an extra-short walk because I was on deadline.

And, last, but certainly not least, our wonderful agent, Stephany Evans of the Imprint Agency, our delightful editor, Jean Lucas, and her editorial assistant, Lane Butler, and the team at Andrews McMeel, without whom none of this would have been possible. You have our heartfelt thanks and gratitude!

INTRODUCTION

WHY WE HAVE DESIGNS ON YOU

Design is an ever-evolving art form, and it's never too early—or too late—to explore your aesthetic sensibilities. It's not just about upgrading your living space—it's about upgrading your life. And we want to show you how.

MEET THE AUTHORS

So, why would you take kitchen design advice from a girl who once set her Easy Bake Oven on fire and a design aficionado who discovered her passion for fashion rescuing a neighbor's discarded lamp from the garbage truck? Let us introduce ourselves!

Janice Anne Costa

As editor of *Kitchen & Bath Design News,* the industry's leading magazine for kitchen dealers and designers, I've spent the past decade exploring beautiful kitchens. Month after month, year after year, I've reviewed hundreds and thousands of designer kitchens, exploring not only their aesthetic appeal, but also what makes them work—or *not* work—for their owners.

Over the past decade, I have been privileged to associate with some of the finest kitchen designers in the country. They continually inspire me with their passion for creating beautiful spaces that truly evoke the personalities of their owners. Not only do these talented designers excel at creating aesthetic masterpieces, they also understand that a key aspect of their job is to make people's homes work better, smarter, and more enjoyably.

Some people think design is frivolous. I believe that anyone who's ever had a home knows better. Your home is your sanctuary, the kitchen the heart of that sanctuary. It should be a room that makes you feel good, comforts you, nourishes your spirit, pleases the eye, and calms the mind. It should be a place that feeds you, body and soul.

People frequently ask me how I decided on this field. Actually, I wasn't born with a passion for design, or for the culinary arts. I learned to cook on an Easy Bake Oven—and some would argue that my cooking skills never evolved much beyond the pursuit of the perfect chocolate cupcake. However, despite my limited culinary talents, I've always had a certain fascination with the kitchen.

Growing up in a large Italian family, I spent much of my childhood in our tiny, cheerful kitchen. I remember stealing tastes of my mom's homemade sauce, fighting with my sisters over who got the bigger piece of cake, feeding vegetables to the dog under the table, baking Christmas cookies in the shapes of angels, and frosting them with colored icing to make them resemble members of our family.

Most of all, I remember living, loving, sharing, and making memories in that warm, happy room. Those memories are still deeply embedded in my psyche. In fact, even today, I can be transported back to childhood with a simple whiff of homemade chicken soup, tangy meat sauce, or marshmallow-topped sweet potatoes.

While I loved our little kitchen, my mom was frustrated by it. The lighting was awful, there was too little storage, counter space was practically nonexistent, and the traffic flow was so poorly designed that the dog was always getting stepped on. "I'm *not* going to die in this kitchen!" was her endless refrain throughout my childhood, and well into my adulthood. Thankfully, after some thirty-eight years, she finally got a kitchen that's as wonderful to work in as it was to grow up in.

I don't believe people should wait thirty-eight years to have a kitchen they can feel good about. I don't believe good design is a luxury.

The kitchen is where we work, play, talk, prepare meals, share food, family, and memories. A beautiful, functional kitchen improves and enriches our lives. It gives us a place to let our hair down and relax; to talk, share, bake cookies; to be, and become. And there's nothing frivolous about that.

In *Everything and the Kitchen Sink,* we hope to inspire you to create your own dream kitchen—not tomorrow, or some day down the road, but now. Because you can beautify your world and simplify your life at any price point. And we can think of no better investment you can make in your home, your family, and your happiness.

Daina Manning

How did I get mixed up with this design stuff? Well, I've always been an amateur decorator. In every dumpy apartment I ever lived in during my starving journalist days in New York City, I would paint, put up shelves and mirrors, staple-gun fabric to walls, and even walk the streets late at night before garbage day looking for cool stuff other people were throwing out.

But my interest really picked up the day I found a lamp. I was walking the dog in Astoria, Queens, when I discovered this 1950s lamp with a two-tiered shade in a leaf pattern. It was just a completely silly piece of design, sitting on the curb, waiting for the garbage man. The lamp actually made me laugh out loud—so what else could I do but take it home? And right then and there, a lifelong passion for twentieth-century design was born.

Now, years later, I still love Art Deco, Modern Retro, and those big, overstuffed, 1940s club chairs. From the ridiculous to the sublime, my place is a testament to retro and vintage.

Today I live in California, where I make short films and write screenplays as well as design stories for a host of publications, including *Kitchen & Bath Design News* and its sister publication, *Design/Build Business*—and I've added all the cool Deco-meets-Mediterranean vintage they have out here to my list of architectural loves.

I was also fortunate enough to marry into a great New England–based family where antiques and expert DIY restoration are a way of life. My in-laws bought an 1800s mansion that was one step away from being condemned and, over twenty years, turned it into a palace. Their accomplishment really demonstrated the importance of preserving architecture—and how to stay true to period style while taking advantage of modern conveniences.

I'd like to help other people find their design bliss, as well. Your environment is so important. An unpleasant one can bring you down with its clutter and drabness. A beautiful one, though, can be your sanctuary and a great source of comfort and inspiration. It can make you feel strong, relaxed, and confident.

Everyone deserves good design. That's true whether you have a million dollars to spend on your home, or can barely afford paint and lumber. Money can't buy good taste, and lack of money can't prevent you from having style.

I also want to tell the truth about remodeling. Never mind the pretty photos, or TV programs that show only the "before" and "after" but rarely the "during" of a project. We hope this guide will help you achieve all your design dreams.

Everything
and the
Kitchen Sink

CHAPTER 1

WHY REMODEL?

The Tragic 1970s Avocado Green Nightmare

You bought that adorable 1970s-style ranch because you love the neighborhood, the school district, the huge backyard, and the big sunny living room. The kitchen, however—well, let's be frank. It's hideous. Sure, it might have been the height of fashion once—back when disco was king. But today, that harvest gold and avocado green color scheme is about as appealing as a man in a powder blue leisure suit.

Neither is your dated kitchen winning any points in terms of function. Increasingly, your

TV tastes drift to HGTV, where you see other people's beautiful stainless steel and granite culinary palaces, and sigh. You know you can't put it off anymore—clearly it's time for action.

Top Ten Reasons to Remodel

Remodeling your kitchen is an integral step to making your house into your dream home. After all, the kitchen, more than any other room in the house, is where you live. It's your refuge from an increasingly hectic world. The kitchen is where you relax, spend time with family, cook, enjoy meals, and entertain friends. A gorgeous, stylish, updated kitchen can not only make your home more appealing, it can also save you time

It's time to get your own spectacular culinary palace. DESIGNER: *Gary White, CMKBD, CID (Kitchen and Bath Design)* PHOTO: *Larry Falke* ◀

and simplify your life. Even better, updating your kitchen is a great investment, since it increases the resale value of your home.

Although your kitchen may be outdated, you might still wonder whether you can afford to renovate. The good news is, you can't afford *not* to. There are a million good reasons for renovating your kitchen, from taking advantage of record-low interest rates and increasing your home's resale value to impressing friends and clients. But, if you're still looking for a way to justify your new kitchen, here is our list of the top ten reasons to remodel.

1. *You are what you eat.*

Are you beginning to worry that the guy at Burger King knows your kids by name? When you try out a new hair color, does the Chinese food delivery guy notice before your spouse does? A new kitchen might just inspire you to spend less time driving through or eating out. Even better, the latest appliances speed up cooking times, and offer all kinds of extras to help you make better-tasting, healthier foods.

2. *Support energy conservation.*

Many older appliances consume enough energy to power a small third-world country. Your parents taught you to clean your plate because kids are starving in Africa. Shouldn't you be equally conscientious about saving energy?

3. *College is over.*

Just because you made it through four years of higher education with only a hot plate and a toaster oven doesn't mean you should cook that way for the rest of your life. You've got a grown-up job and a mortgage now. It's time to live like an adult.

4. *Remodelers need your money more than doctors do.*

Cracked surfaces are havens for dirt and bacteria that can be dangerous to you and your family. Wouldn't you prefer the short-term inconvenience of a renovation (where you at least end up with a brand-new kitchen) to a long hospital stay for food poisoning (where your doctor ends up with a BMW, and all you get is green Jell-O)?

5. *Children shouldn't glow in the dark.*

Modern microwaves/convection ovens are safer and more efficient than those of previous generations—and they won't give your food that weird gummy taste.

6. *Equality of the sexes.*

Your spouse just spent $10,000 on an outdoor grill/smoker combo that puts out enough BTUs to be visible on NASA satellite images. Now, it's your turn!

7. *You're gifted.*

Why does the gorgeous china you received as a wedding gift reside in a scratched-up cabinet with a missing knob? Isn't it time your kitchen matched its beautiful accessories?

8. Fire is so seventeenth century.

Well, actually, a powerful gas range is still a pretty great thing—but other parts of the cooking experience have come a long way since the basics. The latest advances in technology are almost magical, so why not take advantage of them?

9. Change is a good thing.

Unlike your parents, your boss, your spouse, or your children, your kitchen actually *can* be changed. And once improvements are made,

they're permanent—no need to maintain them with nagging, bribes, threats, or marriage counseling.

10. That marriage you save may be your own.

Are you addicted to HGTV? Does your spouse threaten to redo the home à la that NASCAR theme they did on *Monster House* if you subscribe to *just one more* decorating magazine? Maybe it's time to stop dreaming about that ultimate kitchen, and do it, already!

But seriously, why do people take the plunge into the kitchen remodeling adventure?

Soft neutrals and stainless steel are hallmarks of new millennium design. **DESIGNER:** *John Sofio (Built, Inc.)* **PHOTO:** *Courtesy of Lone Pine Pictures* ▶

A kitchen that's designed to be accessible and easy to use has a universal appeal that never goes out of style. **DESIGNER:** *Mary Jo Peterson, CKD, CBD, CMG (MJ Peterson Designs)* ◀

These days, your kitchen doesn't have to be an antique, or a disaster, to warrant an upgrade. The luxury kitchen is one of American homeowners' most fervent dreams.

While a top-of-the-line kitchen can cost considerably more than a car, many homeowners are happily signing on the dotted line for large loans to make that dream come true. Why go all the way with your kitchen?

■ *You're a homebody and proud of it.*
The fabulous kitchen is a centerpiece of the overall trend of "cocooning." In these hectic times, people are finding greater satisfaction in returning to home and hearth, spending quiet time with their families, and transforming their home into a combination refuge and castle. When your kitchen gives you that warm and fuzzy feeling, the world seems like a safer place. So why not turn your kitchen into the true heart of your home?

■ *It's your corporate dining room and party spot.*
More and more people are working from home, often putting money into lovely, tasteful home offices.

Piles of paper atop chipped and faded countertops may be fine if no one's around to see them, but they're no good if your home is going to make a professional statement about who you are (or who you want people to think you are!). A gorgeous, well-designed kitchen says you're sophisticated, style-conscious, and

Before redesigning your kitchen, think about how long you plan to stay in your home.

■ **Less than three years:** Go with a simple layout. Opt for easy, inexpensive upgrades and classic colors that will appeal to the greatest number of users.

■ **Three to seven years:** Buy quality brand names but avoid top-of-the-line, cutting-edge technology that will likely come down in price before you have a chance to recoup its value. Keep the style of the kitchen in line with that of the home, and focus on value add-ons that will make your life easier—cabinet pull-outs and roll-out shelves, for instance.

■ **Seven years or longer:** Focus less on what a future owner may enjoy, and more on creating an environment you'll enjoy living and working in. Invest in appliances that cook the way you do, surfaces that are durable and easy to maintain, and a design that suits your family's needs. Remember, many people who plan to upgrade from their starter home in seven years end up staying in their homes closer to ten or twelve years—so be sure you go for a kitchen you can not just live with, but love, too. ■

ahead of the times—or at least not stuck in 1977 and living on TV dinners.

Likewise, home entertaining is on the rise. And where do people congregate during the party? The kitchen, of course! Having a great-looking kitchen is a must, even for people who cater everything. After all, appearances count.

■ *Cooking is your passion.*

Gourmet cooks, on the other hand, look at the people whose gorgeous, professional-quality range goes unused for months at a time and think—*what are they, nuts?* For them, it's not form but function that truly counts.

Gourmet cooking is an increasingly popu-

lar hobby among both men and women. In fact, it's the male cooks who frequently go all out with techno-gadgets such as Internet-enabled refrigerators and professional-style cooktops with more power than the Incredible Hulk. But whether you like to bake, grill, sear, or stir-fry, there's a host of exciting new cooking options that can help you make better tasting, healthier food. So if cooking is your passion, a new set of culinary bells and whistles is a great reason to update your kitchen.

■ ***You have the cash, and you want to show it off.*** Okay, admit it, you want to impress people. You want the best in life and are willing to pay for it. You love your Mercedes and your Armanis.

These days, the must-have status symbol is a fabulous kitchen with unique features that friends, neighbors, and your annoying cousin Donna will be sure to envy. You're willing to get out there and find the latest, greatest thing to make your kitchen an important design statement.

Sell, Sell, Sell

On the other hand, perhaps you bought your house with an eye toward resale. Or maybe you just need an excuse to rationalize getting the new kitchen of your dreams—and "because I want a built-in wok" doesn't cut it with your spouse, who'd rather invest the money in a new Jeep.

Either way, the good news is that renovating your kitchen makes excellent financial sense. According to the National Association of Realtors, a remodeled kitchen boosts the value of a home by thousands of dollars. In fact, some industry sources now claim that a new kitchen can recoup between 94 percent and 114 percent of its cost during resale.

So, what's the best way to maximize resale? To begin with, look for quality products and brand names you trust. If you're thinking in terms of resale, avoid cutting-edge technology with all the bells and whistles. If you can't bear to pass on all those exciting electronic kitchen gizmos, buy only those you can take with you when you move.

Stick with an accessible layout that appeals to the maximum number of users. Built-in safety features—rounded corners on an island, appliances with automatic shutoffs or antiscald faucets—are always a good idea. These appeal to everyone, and make the house more saleable.

If you're thinking about resale, go with a soft, classic color scheme rather than something bold or dramatic. Soft neutrals and stainless steel are good bets if you want your design to have lasting appeal.

But what if you've decided that white shows too much dirt, black is too dark, stainless is too sterile, and bisque makes you think of soup? If you absolutely *must* have color, use it as an accent, in areas that are easily changed out. This way you can enjoy your favorite color right now, without sacrificing resale later on.

If you plan to stay in your house for a long time, go for a kitchen you love, such as this light-hearted retro look.

DESIGNER: *Ellen Cheever, CMKBD, ASID (Ellen Cheever and Associates)* ◀

When planning for resale, it's smart to avoid extremes (no hand-painted tile murals depicting four generations of your family). But don't obsess, either. Even if you only spend a few years in your home, a lot of that time will be spent in the kitchen. So be sure to create a room you can feel good about.

Your Kitchen, Forever

On the other hand, maybe resale value doesn't mean much to you because you don't plan to move—ever. Perhaps you were emotionally scarred for life when the movers hijacked your furniture during the last move. Or maybe you can't bear to give up that oversized walk-in closet with the built-in shoe shelves that would hold all of Imelda Marcos's shoe collection and then some. Or perhaps you have kids who have finally moved out and you cherish your empty nest.

If this is your house for the rest of your life, you want the kitchen you've always dreamed of.

So, forget the trends and go for what you love.

Something Old, Something New

Restoring an authentic period home has become a passion for many—and these days, there are more reasons to do so than ever.

You may love your 1930s Spanish-style home with its imaginative archways and charming wood floors. Unfortunately, the kitchen's authentic tile work is crumbling, discolored, and a haven for germs. You want to keep that cool old gas stove with the built-in clock—but the layout of the cabinetry makes storage a chore. Retro vibe or no retro vibe, it sure would be nice to have roll-outs and pull-outs, not to mention a center island. And then there are the recycling bins and the water purifier. All those modern conveniences, and nowhere to put them.

Luckily, you don't have to sacrifice authentic period style to get new millennium technology. These days, you can replace that 1930s-style faucet with a brand-new one that has the same look. Manufacturers have developed a wide variety of products that evoke styles from any and all eras, ensuring that your kitchen will retain its vintage charm—while adding efficiency and modern technology to the mix.

The Green Kitchen

You can even use saving the environment as a way to justify your kitchen remodel. People have become more environmentally conscious in recent years, motivated by a fervent desire to save the planet from an avalanche of garbage and muck. Or maybe recycling is mandatory in your neck of the woods, and if you don't do it, you get a ticket. So where do you put those three unsightly garbage bins, anyway? This is where cabinet storage systems come into play, with large pull-out bins that house two or more garbage cans.

Likewise, water quality has increasingly become an issue. A lot of city water tastes awful and it also contains God-knows-what impurities. People have increasingly turned to bottled water, but hauling it around can be a real hassle. Water filtration systems are another facet of the ultimate kitchen, providing instant and plentiful clean water, either directly through the faucet, or through the refrigerator.

You know you don't like to use up that pricey bottled stuff for cooking vegetables, making coffee, or filling up pet dishes. But, with a filtration system, you've got all that covered.

The New Millennium Family

Of course, one of the biggest reasons people remodel is because today's families have changed, both in form and function. Unfortunately, many kitchens are still better suited to the *Leave It to Beaver* families of yesteryear.

Two-career couples are on the rise, making speed cooking a must. Singles of both sexes may experiment with gourmet cooking on the weekend and rely on smart appliances to program their dinner during the week. Kids who once waited patiently for meals now frequently help prepare them.

Fortunately, the great variety of kitchen products today reflects the wide range of consumers and their different needs, and remodeling lets you choose exactly what's right for you.

While gourmet cooks want the ultimate professional cooking experience, overworked two-career families just need their food fast—without resorting to actual fast food. A single homeowner may want a cozy, comfortable kitchen with everything stored within easy reach, or a high-tech haven with appliances that can be programmed from the office using a computer or cell phone.

In the new millennium kitchen, that little phone area may need to be expanded to include a complete computer station, perhaps stylishly matching the wood species and door style of your kitchen cabinets.

Whatever your family setup, a kitchen designed around your family's specific needs and lifestyles can improve your life, save you time, and help bring your family together.

So, there you have it. There are a million good reasons to remodel, and one of them is right for you.

Improved heat-management

technology is just one of

the many advantages avail-

able to the new millennium

family. ▲

CHAPTER 2
DESIGN FOR LIVING

Good design is as much about how you live as how things look. So, if you truly want to make the most of your new kitchen, you really need to think about how you're going to use it. Take a good, hard look at your cooking habits, your eating preferences, your entertainment needs, your messiness quotient, and what you really use your kitchen for. Then, think about the things you don't use your kitchen for that you'd like to. What would make your kitchen more usable? Extra counter space? More accessible storage? Updated appliances? An island or breakfast bar?

Whether you plan to hire a designer, work with a home center, or do it yourself, first get some ideas together about what you really want and need.

Get your choices and goals clearly in your mind before you encounter people who want to sell you stuff. Because everyone has their own agenda—even really nice, talented people who genuinely want to help you get a fabulous kitchen.

Maybe the home center is overstocked on a particular line of appliances at the moment, so everyone there is hyping the stuff. Perhaps your high-end designer is pushing you toward European Minimalist Contemporary because that's the style he loves with all his heart, and he wants to see cold steely clean lines throughout the land. Maybe your designer is overworked and is steering you toward Mediterranean because it's a popular style where you live. Of course it doesn't hurt that she's done a ton of Mediterranean kitchens, and if you pick that, she'll be able to do your project in her sleep.

All design is a quandary of form and function, but in the kitchen, function wins. If you have a gorgeous space that doesn't really work for you, it's going to be like those stunning designer shoes that seemed like such a good idea at the time. Unfortunately, the very pointy toe squishes your foot, and every time you put them on, you feel uncomfortable. So you don't really wear them that much, and, truth be told, those shoes are kind of a disappointment.

If you're a zillionaire whose kitchen will never be touched by anyone except the catering staff, you can make a "trophy kitchen" design statement without thinking about how you're actually going to be using the space. But otherwise, your kitchen has to work with how you really live, not the fantasy of how you think you *should* live.

A Kitchen to Fit Your Lifestyle

Yes, it's a quiz. But we're not going to grade you on this, or brand you with some label like "Urban Perfectionist Striver." Everyone is an

It's important to think about how you're going to really use your kitchen space. Here, a well-organized cooktop and sink area simplifies kitchen functions. PHOTO: *Courtesy of Wolf* ◄

individual, and there are no right answers when it comes to how you use your kitchen. Just think about your kitchen space as you read on.

1. ***Which of the following best describes a typical dinner at your house?***
   A. Chicken cordon bleu, a salad of spring greens with goat cheese and pecans, a homemade mousse cake, and a charming bottle of sauvignon blanc.
   B. Homemade stir-fry with organic vegetables, brown rice, tofu, and Thai peanut sauce.
   C. At our house, it's all about speed and convenience—lots of ordering in.
   D. Family-size Chicken Helper.
   E. Big-ass steaks on the outdoor grill, plus fries.

2. ***Which of the following best describes the contents of your cabinets?***
   A. The spices are alphabetized, the glasses are grouped together by casual, party, and formal, and the canned goods have a color-code system.
   B. Delivery menus.
   C. Chock-full of basics like tuna, soup, pasta, and rice.
   D. Eleven different kinds of hot sauce with names like the Exterminator, Sweet Pain, and Cajun Whoop-Ass. And not much else.

3. ***How many people are likely to be in your kitchen at the same time?***
   A. My spouse and I love to plan meals together, so sometimes one of us does the entrée, the other the side dish.
   B. Too many! All the time! It's not like we have the room, either. I keep telling the kids to do their homework somewhere else, but do they listen? And of course, the dog has to follow them everywhere they go, so that's another body in the way.
   C. None. It's just me, and I'm not home that much.

4. ***The one thing you don't have now and you wish for is:***
   A. More space! I bought this condo for the view from the living room window, but, man, this kitchenette is getting to me.
   B. A Viking range! I see that baby in the window of the kitchen showroom every day, and it's just calling to me. I know I can do such great stuff, if only . . .
   C. I want an appliance where you just put raw ingredients in it and it prepares the meal for you. I guess they haven't made one of those yet, huh?

Messy people need plenty of storage space! **DESIGNER:** *Steven Naphtali (Kitchen Expressions of Short Hills)* **PHOTO:** *Daniel Aubry, New York* ◀

Help for the Neatness Challenged

Your ideal self lives in a perfect minimalist kitchen where shiny stainless steel meets a Zen-like natural concrete countertop—just like that incredible space you saw in *Metropolitan Home*.

In real life, you're a single mom who doesn't get home until seven most nights and you have two teenagers who need to make their own after-school snacks.

Are you kidding? That stainless steel will never look fingerprint free and perfect. (Well, maybe for the first forty-five minutes after the cleaning service comes.) That concrete will get a mysterious but permanent stain the first week.

Or you're attracted to those very ornate, Old World "my kitchen escaped in a time machine from the court of Queen Elizabeth I" designs with carved wood and little nooks and crannies all over the place. But you're also prone to exuberant omelets that inevitably cause bits of oil to fly every which way. Think of what those charming little Enkeboll carvings are going to look like two years from now, when you'll fervently be wishing you'd gone with easy-to-clean flat panel doors.

Being messy is not a crime. We, your guides through the wonderful world of kitchen remodeling, are frequently messy (especially when we're on deadline!). But please admit this to yourself and plan your kitchen design accordingly.

THE BIG QUESTION—
How Messy Are You, Honestly?

1. *When you have a holiday party and someone spills red wine on your countertop, how long will that spill stay there?*
   A. Three minutes
   B. Three hours
   C. Until sometime in the future when you or your spouse utters the magic words, "Honey, the kitchen is disgusting, we have to do something about it *now!*"

2. *Your child's secret nickname is:*
   A. The Princess
   B. Calamity Jane
   C. The Tasmanian Devil

3. *How often do you do the dishes?*
   A. Well, I rinse them immediately after I use them, and then they go to a staging area, where I rinse them more thoroughly before putting them in the dishwasher.
   B. Once a day, more or less.
   C. Before anyone comes over and sees what a slob I really am.

4. *The strangest thing that's ever been spilled in your kitchen is:*
   A. That peculiar Indian chutney.
   B. Well, the kids were all going to be vampires for Halloween and they tried to make fake blood . . .
   C. Motor oil. Don't ask.

You get the picture. So for you, our messy brothers and sisters:

RULES FOR HAPPY (QUASI) MESSY LIVING

1. For both metal and paint, shiny surfaces equal fingerprints. The brushed, satin, or otherwise textured surface is your friend. Embrace it in as many applications as possible.

2. For countertops, paradoxically, an unshiny (honed) surface equals higher maintenance. Generally, the more sealed and polished natural stone is, the less you have to worry. Porous surfaces are also higher maintenance. If you are messy, please choose a solid surface or engineered stone for your countertop.

3. Even well-sealed grout is harder to clean than a flat surface. Be careful with tile of any sort, especially on horizontal surfaces.

4. Open shelves and glass doors are a great way to make that long row of cabinets look more interesting. The only problem is you can see what's on the shelves, and that may not be pretty. So, use these as you would a spicy condiment—sparingly. Consider adding spaces where you can just push stuff in and close the door.

5. You also want a lot of spaces where you can apply that old "a place for everything and everything in its place" adage. Cabinet organizers have come a long way since the lazy Susan. Organizers actually *do* help you stay organized, so try to make room in your budget for them.

6. Decor extremes tend to be higher maintenance than the middle ground. For example, very minimalist and modern is hard to take care of because everything has to be put away, and the surfaces can show prints. Extremely fouffy and ornate is also hard to take care of because of all the little bitty nooks that need to be kept clean. Consider something you like in between these two extremes.

7. Real stainless steel is a fingerprint nightmare (polished more so than brushed or otherwise textured). Appliances are now available in stainless steel look-alikes that are more forgiving to grimy little fingers.

9. Avoid crevices. Dirt will hang out at your place, because it intuitively knows it's found a home there. So, consider an integrated undermount sink instead of a drop-in one.

A Kitchen to Fit the Rest of Your Home

WORK TRIANGLE OR BERMUDA TRIANGLE?

Conventional wisdom in kitchen planning says you should have the work triangle, i.e., the walking path between the refrigerator, stove, and sink.

For instance, in your basic galley layout, the sink and refrigerator would be against one wall, while the range would be on the other.

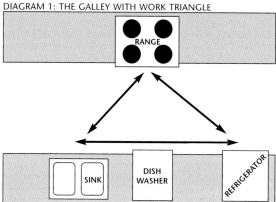

DIAGRAM 1: THE GALLEY WITH WORK TRIANGLE

8. No matter how small your space, how limited your budget, or what you have to do, if you're messy, you must have a good, powerful dishwasher. You just must.

Another basic layout is the L Shape.

DIAGRAM 2: THE L SHAPE WITH WORK TRIANGLE

For small spaces, you have the big-city kitchenette layout, with the kitchen based against one wall. Sadly, no triangle for you.

DIAGRAM 3: THE KITCHENETTE WITH NO WORK TRIANGLE

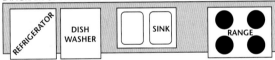

But what if your kitchen is much bigger than this, and includes an island, passages into a great room space, and an overall more complex arrangement?

The traditional work triangle also assumes there's only one cook, and that cook is preparing a traditional meal—where you're taking raw food out of the fridge, prepping it in some manner, and then cooking it on the stove.

Is this how cooking happens around your house, or is it more, people in and out, this way and that? One person is microwaving a snack while two others are pairing up to get the roast in the oven so it will be done for dinner at eight. Or you're standing next to the refrigerator when making a salad because it's easier to toss the veggies back in the bin when you're done.

Modular Design

How many people in your family cook, and what's the maximum number of cooks that you customarily have in your kitchen? If the answer is more than one, you're going to want to configure your kitchen differently than the old work triangle formula. Instead, think of multiple triangles, or perhaps work modules.

Your designer, or your DIY software program, will be able to help you work out the traffic flow for a large kitchen. But here are some ideas.

THE VEGGIE MODULE

If you're dedicated to the healthy, green, and leafy approach to cuisine, wouldn't it be convenient to have a second, smaller refrigerator somewhere for just your fresh vegetables? Maybe a little veggie station with a second sink and food prep area, so one of you could make the salad and get the zucchini ready for the steamer while the other person tackles the main course?

Sub-Zero originated refrigerator-in-a-drawer modules for just this purpose—so you can put your refrigeration wherever it's most convenient. However, if the price of such a system gives you immediate shortness of breath,

The beverage station is a great way of organizing your kitchen, especially if you entertain a lot. DESIGNER: *Gail Drury, CKD/CBD (Drury Designs)* PHOTO: *Kristine Wolff, Kristine Wolff Photography* ▶

don't fret. It's possible to take the basic idea of refrigerated storage in more than one place in the kitchen and implement it less expensively, for instance, by incorporating a generic undercounter fridge in an island.

THE BEVERAGE STATION

It used to be people had proper bars and cocktails at five, and some still do. But for a whirling dervish house where drinks are more likely to be juice boxes and sodas consumed on the run, consider a beverage station. Again, the concept could range from high end (brand-name temperature-controlled wine cooler, built-in beer tap, stainless-steel bar sink, minifridge for sodas and water) to economical (Pier One wine rack above undercounter refrigerator).

Kitchens have been getting bigger in recent years, but wider aisles are particularly important when you have multiple cooks. A forty-eight-inch aisle ensures that two people can pass each other carrying hot plates of goodies without resulting in screams, scalding, or a traumatic journey to the emergency room. If you have a small kitchen, it's better to opt for a smaller island than short-change the moving-around room. Likewise, be sure that when the oven or refrigerator door is open, there's still clearance room. ■

THE INSTANT MEAL MODULE

If you're a family of workaholics, save money on fancy cooking appliance add-ons and invest it in things you'll really need. How about an extra freezer filled with heat-and-serve meal options? If people are always standing in line to use the microwave around your place—why not avoid gridlock and get two on opposite sides of the kitchen?

THE PET MODULE

Your pets deserve their own module, too. If your enormous dogs drink enough water to float the *Queen Mary* and are always slobbering it all over, a corner with a floor-mounted sink would give them fresh water all the time, without hauling those bowls over to the sink and back seventeen times a day.

Come to think of it, how many times have you tripped over, or stepped into, their food bowls this week? A little alcove to tuck the bowls into would solve this problem once and for all. And a giant metal pull-out bin would be a handy place to store that forty-pound bag of dog food. Add a basic drawer for bones, chew toys, and doggie vitamins, and you're set.

Cook It Like a Man: Tips for a Testosterone-Friendly Kitchen

It's not the 1950s anymore, and guys have discovered that cooking is a smart thing to learn, for more reasons than one.

Top Ten Reasons for Guys to Cook

1. When your wife is not watching, you can stand in front of 50,000-BTU gas range, play with burners, and scream, *"More power!"*

2. Cooking a gourmet meal for a hot girlfriend is actually more effective than flowers for getting her in the mood.

3. That month when your wife had her big multinational sales conference and your kids were actually crying, begging you for something to eat other than pizza again. That was sad.

4. Cooking makes you feel like a wild, creative, primal man, like Emeril. Bam!

5. Helping with Thanksgiving dinner scored you major points with mom and enabled you to lord it over your annoying, sexist brother-in-law.

6. Do you know how many cool techno-gadgets you can buy if you're a gourmet cook? Especially since you already have the giant plasma screen, iPod, iSight, and TiVo. What else are you going to shop for?

7. You're able to play the King of the World Grill Master role all year round, not just during summer barbecue.

8. The cook gets to pick the menu. That means no cilantro or goat cheese, ever!

9. Because you never know when you're going to have to go to the mattresses.

10. You don't catch grief for having a drink the minute you get home—you're cooking, for heaven's sake, and the wine is for the coq au vin!

To make your kitchen testosterone-friendly, remember these pointers:

■ Men are generally taller than women. So keep your height in mind when installing the vent hood over the range, the pot rack, the task light over the island, and other things you could bonk your head on.

■ When going for the gadgets, don't forget the interior of the cabinets. That stainless-steel pull-out thing that brings all the pots and pans out of the back cabinet as if by magic is pretty cool.

■ Admit it. When you're cooking steaks out by the pool, you enjoy having an audience. So why not make the same configuration for your kitchen arena? Get that sink and/or cooktop away from the back wall and on the island, facing an area where your guests can hang out, have a drink, and admire your skill with a sauté pan.

■ There's an old joke that women want to watch a $500 TV on a $5,000 couch, whereas men want to watch a $5,000 TV on a $500 couch. This generalization is somewhat true in the kitchen as well. So make sure your budget includes the things that are the most important for each of you, and leave some of the extras out, if necessary. Don't go completely nuts with the gadgets and the appliances. Honestly, how often can you really use that built-in deep fryer without becoming a heart attack waiting to happen? But don't let your wife talk you into the overpriced cherub-orchid carvings and triple glaze on the cabinets, either.

Lost in Space

Houses are getting larger, but the number of rooms is decreasing. Welcome to the great room concept. What was formerly the kitchen, the dining room, and the family room has metamorphosed into one huge space. This may also include the home entertainment center and a computer station for bill paying, homework, and the like.

How does this affect your kitchen plan? Well, it would look kind of weird if you had a homey, artful-clutter Country kitchen looking out onto your Modernist I-am-a-suave-upscale-urban-dweller home theater setup, wouldn't it?

The great room space needs to work as a whole, both in terms of look and traffic flow.

This is not to say that you have to go whole hog and continue identical cabinets throughout all these areas. Coordination, however, is a good thing. Perhaps use one door style, but different wood species and stains. Or use a striking dark cherry wood as the accent through-line, but complement it with different door styles and looks to mark off the different rooms.

If you're doing a major-league remodel, different ceiling heights can also be used to separate spaces without putting in a wall.

The increasingly popular great room area needs to have a coordinated look between kitchen and entertainment room.

DESIGNER: *Carlos Mindeau, AIA (Metropolitan Design)*

PHOTO: *Sam Fentress* ◀

A Space for Mini-Me

Maybe your space problem is not how to coordinate it, but how to get more of it. Many beautiful big-city condos have kitchens smaller than the one on the International Space Station. But small can be beautiful, and efficient, too.

■ You may not think you have room for a dishwasher, but you do. See "Your Friend, the Dishwasher" in Chapter 7 for more details.

■ Here's a radical thought: Maybe you actually *don't* need a regular oven. A small countertop cooktop plus a speed-cook microwave/oven and some kind of grilling appliance like the George Foreman could be enough for you.

■ A wide array of products—microwaves, little TVs, racks for stemware storage—can be wall-mounted under the top row of cabinets these days, or under-mounted to the bottom of the cabinets themselves. Bring your cabinet height up by six inches to a foot, and a wealth of options open up to you, without taking up valuable countertop space.

■ Think European. Kitchens in Europe have less space than in the United States, so

Tip

If you're planning on tearing out some walls and making your kitchen part of a great room space, pay attention to the sound and light aspects of your room. This is especially true if you're going for a clean, modern look with a lot of wood and steel. Without carpeting, drapes, and other materials that absorb sound, your beautiful room could sound like an echo chamber. ■

European manufacturers have come up with some amazing and stylish storage options. For instance, pull-outs that are tall and countertop-deep, but only six inches wide, will enable you to store a huge number of jars and cans in the dead space between two banks of cabinets.

■ If your present large refrigerator contains milk for coffee, three containers of leftover Szechuan delivery, a bottle of chardonnay, and a bag of ready-to-eat salad whose expiration date was, sadly, two weeks ago—*why* do you need that huge refrigerator? An undercounter model may serve your needs just fine, and free up lot of space.

Station to Station

Here are some hints for making the information area (otherwise known as the family bill-paying desk, the computer station, or the communication module) of your great room work more effectively:

- Everyone who uses this area should have their own drawer, and keep their own stuff in it, otherwise there will be continuous yelling and accusations (you took my pen! I did not!). Anything left outside of said drawer is fair game.

- Take the time to find out where your family's real work areas are. Don't assume the space you set up when you first moved in is still effective. Technology has changed, and your tasks may have changed. For instance: Is anyone actually using the desktop computer? Increasingly, people are gravitating to laptops even though they have a properly set up computer station with all the trimmings. If only one person in the family is still using the big desktop, perhaps that computer could be moved to his or her room, freeing up group space for something else?

- If you do have one desktop computer that everyone uses, make sure your computer station isn't rigidly customized to fit just that model of computer. Remember when the iMacs came out and they were a whole different shape? You don't know what kind of computer you're going to be putting in there three years from now. Likewise, you might want the communication module for other things, so make sure your plan is flexible.

- You don't need a bill-paying surface if you actually pay your bills online with your laptop. However, you do need a spot to store the box or accordion file you put the bills in.

- You do need a "dump spot." This is the place where everyone dumps their keys, the mail, sunglasses, the dog leash, and other items. Often, the dump spot is in the kitchen, or around the computer station. The dump spot needs to be in the place the family actually uses. An arbitrarily assigned spot will not work, because people will naturally migrate to the spot that is most convenient. Think of where everyone in the family leaves their small but important belongings, and make the communication module go there if at all possible.

- Make sure you have enough electrical outlets for things like iPods, Palm Pilots, cell phones, games, and other electronics that need their batteries recharged. Your power strip(s) should also be accessible without having to burrow down in that area behind the desk with all the cords and dust.

- Make sure your station has some kind of bulletin-board arrangement for attaching phone messages, grocery lists, and other important notes.

- The technology in those advanced pull-outs that bring pots and pans out from the far reaches of the base cabinets can also be applied to the computer work area. If you really don't want that printer sitting out there all day, every day, there's a way of tucking it—as if by magic!—into its own little cabinet.

That's Entertainment: Tips for Incorporating Home Entertainment Centers

The home entertainment center is not, strictly speaking, part of the kitchen. It can, however, be part of a great room arrangement. If you're going this route, you might as well coordinate by using the same cabinet line you have in your kitchen. Here are some things to keep in mind:

- Make sure the person you're buying your electronic equipment from communicates with your kitchen designer during planning and installation. Entertainment centers have specific requirements for outlets, dimensions of A/V equipment, and the like. You don't want a beautiful built-in wall unit that's six inches smaller than your new plasma screen TV.

- Think outside the box, literally. Many terrific entertainment centers are constructed from kitchen cabinets. This approach allows you to customize in ways you can't with stock entertainment wall units. For instance, how about a pull-out bin in the base where your kids can keep all their video game accessories?

- Make sure your plan includes room for growth. For example, you're an enthusiastic purchaser of previously viewed DVDs. You may have 100 now, but five years from now, you'll have 400+. Where are you going to put them all?

- Look carefully at the lighting in your kitchen vis à vis your TV. Does the lighting over the island make weird alien spaceship dots on your screen? Likewise, you don't want to have to close all the shades in the kitchen to watch the morning news while having breakfast.

- Decide on the major components of your home theater system *before* you design the wall unit. You should have built-in flexibility, but remember you can't go from a huge, boxy, megascreen projection TV to a flat plasma screen without major changes in the cabinet configuration.

- Where is your beverage station located? If DVD-watching is a big thing with your family, why not make a movie station in the great room area connecting the kitchen and entertainment room? Consider adding a minifridge for drinks and a small microwave for popcorn.

- Remember that every component in your home entertainment system generates heat, and there needs to be adequate ventilation above and behind the components to allow for cooling.

- Mind your speaker placement. You need a certain degree of separation between speakers, and they should be equidistant from your listening position, or else your stereo won't be balanced. This gets even more complicated if you want surround sound. Consult your stereo professional for details.

- Keep electronics away from kitchen appliances and accompanying smoke, grease, and heat.

- Home entertainment electronics have to be on a different electrical circuit from kitchen appliances to avoid interference from appliance motors. A/V systems are sensitive, so make sure you plan your electrical outlets accordingly.

Okay, you've thought about how you live, how you cook, how you eat, and how you entertain. You know what your existing kitchen space is like, and you know what you need to make your new kitchen work for your lifestyle. So now it's time to start planning how you can create that dream kitchen—one that will fulfill all your needs.

CHAPTER 3
PLANNING YOUR KITCHEN: THE ROAD TO KITCHEN NIRVANA

Remodeling your kitchen is a major undertaking that generally demands healthy investments of time, money, and stress—think root canal that lasts a month instead of a few hours, except there's no anesthesia involved.

But, wait, you say. This chapter is supposed to be about nirvana. This doesn't sound like fun at all. And anyway, your neighbor has a beautiful new kitchen that *she* says was a dream come true, from beginning to end. Is she lying?

Probably not. It may just be that she's only remembering the end result. After all, when you ask a new mother how her new baby girl is, does she tell you what a nightmare the labor was? Or does she rhapsodize about the miraculous experience of childbirth to the point where one might wonder why, if it was so rapturous, it required an epidural and still resulted in fourteen hours of screaming, panting, and death threats against her husband?

Whether it's childbirth, a long-worked-for promotion, or a new kitchen, when we achieve the dream, we tend to forget the pain of getting there. This is a good thing to remind yourself of when you're actually in the tear-out stage of a renovation.

Of course someone, somewhere really did have a kitchen remodel that went perfectly from beginning to end, without so much as a moment of inconvenience. Someone, somewhere is also married to Mel Gibson. That someone, unfortunately, is not one of the authors.

What You're in For

Even the most successful kitchen designers admit that the process, although vastly rewarding, can be a bit rocky while getting there. Because, let's face it, having your home torn apart, your kitchen unusable for days or weeks, and strangers parading through your house can be more than a little inconvenient. However, the end result is well worth the trouble. If you can ride out the temporary insanity, before you know it, you, too, will be saying, "I love my beautiful new kitchen . . . it's a dream come true!"

TIME

How long does the process take? Remodeling can take anywhere from a couple of days, say, for a new countertop, to three months or more for a gut-and-start-from-scratch architectural redesign.

Product ordering can add even more time to the process. Some products require lead times of up to nine months. Adding windows, rewiring electrical, moving plumbing, or changing the overall blueprint of the room can also add time to the project.

Even the season can impact the time frame. Remodelers tend to be busiest in the spring and summer, so you can sometimes get faster service if you schedule your job off-season. However, uncertain weather can also present its own set of delays.

So, how do you figure out how long *your* kitchen will take? Once you know what you're having done, you'll want to get several estimates. These should give you a good ballpark time frame.

If time is an issue, ask your designer what you can do to speed up the process. It might be as simple as ordering a different cabinet line, or leaving a window where it is. And, don't forget, if you change your mind about what you want in your kitchen—you've decided to replace your countertops or move that window after all—you've just changed the time frame. ■

Finally, recognize that all good things require an investment of time. Being in too much of a rush can jeopardize your long-term satisfaction.

So, Why Does It Take So Long, Anyway?

People who are frequently late claim that time is relative. Nowhere is this more true than in remodeling, where meeting planned schedules generally requires an alignment of planets, stars and cosmic events the likes of which happen about as often as Halley's Comet.

Why is it, you may wonder, that *you* can manage to coordinate a twelve-hour workday, soccer practice for Susie, day care for Jessie, and multiple trips to the dentist, vet, and grocery store, and yet your remodeler can't manage to show up until 3:30 on the day he told you he'd be there at 7:00 a.m.?

While your remodeler may, indeed, be trying to drive you crazy (or, more likely, has taken on more work than he can handle), the process itself is actually more complicated than you might think. A kitchen remodel requires an enormous amount of coordination, and each element relies on the next for the process to run smoothly. So, if someone mismeasures the dimensions by half an inch, or a snowstorm causes your cabinets to ship late, or your installer gets the flu, the whole project is now thrown off course. Since designers and installers work on multiple projects simultaneously, all with tight schedules, a problem with any other project can also impact your own time schedule.

Furthermore, installations are not an exact science. Frequently, there's no way to know a problem exists until it's exposed when a wall comes down, a sink comes out, or a floor gets pulled up. These can all create additional delays.

Of course that's not particularly comforting when you spend three days with no floor, or there is a gaping hole in the wall where the window is supposed to be. But it's important to keep perspective, and remember that the upheaval is temporary. Long after you've forgotten the mess and chaos, you'll be enjoying your new kitchen.

People frequently ask, What is the best way to avoid delays? The best thing, of course, is to assume things will take longer than the initial estimate, and plan accordingly. If your spouse is always an hour late to everything, do you tell him the surprise birthday party for your mom that starts at eight actually starts at

The best kitchens are installed with care and an eye for detail. **DESIGNER:** *John Sofio (Built, Inc.)* **PHOTO:** *Courtesy of Lone Pine Pictures* ▲

eight—and then fight about missing the surprise for the next twenty years? Or, do you tell him it starts at seven and hope he actually has his act together by eight?

STRESS

Murphy's law is a rule of life, but it's particularly applicable to remodeling. How many days can you stand having the entire contents of your kitchen cabinets spread out in the den, while King Kong–sized boxes take over your living room?

How long can you hold out after being awakened at 7:00 a.m. each day by those tool-belted fellas who take over your house, whistle the same song for ten hours straight, and stomp dust all over your Persian carpet? What if your dog can't stand it anymore and bites one of 'em?

TIPS FOR KEEPING YOUR REMODELING JOB ON SCHEDULE

In the kitchen remodeling business, delays are often inevitable. However, you can help keep things on schedule by following these tips.

1. **Get organized from the beginning,** and stay organized. A remodeling project is a major undertaking that requires time, thought, and planning. Even if flying by the seat of your pants is a way of life for you, this will *not* work for a kitchen remodel. There are simply too many moving parts. Planning ahead is essential.

2. **Get everything on paper,** especially if you're working with others. People are busy and can forget details. So, don't assume when you discussed the way the floor warps slightly a month ago, that your remodeler will remember it—when he's in the middle of tearing out your floor—weeks later. A written agreement not only provides legal protection, it can also provide a valuable memory prompt.

3. **Communicate clearly and regularly** with everyone involved in the process. Clear communication will keep everyone on the same page in terms of expectations, progress, and potential problems.

4. **Be flexible.** When unexpected problems arise, it's sometimes necessary to arrange an unscheduled visit from a plumber, electrician, or contractor. If you can be flexible about your own schedule, it makes it easier to get someone in fast and this helps keep the delays minimal.

5. **If you're doing it yourself, measure everything twice,** or better yet, three times. It's easier to do it right the first time than to fix it later.

6. **Work with professionals.** Get recommendations, and check credentials. And don't just look at pictures of the jobs they completed—get references from satisfied customers. A picture may be worth a thousand words, but talking to a customer who lived through the process is far more telling.

7. **Make payments on time.** When you're late on payments, your project can get bumped to the back of the line.

8. **Never give anyone cash without getting a signed receipt.**

If you've never tried yoga or meditation but always wanted to, now might be a good time to start. It's also a good idea to first discuss the process with your family so everyone knows what to expect.

One of the biggest causes of stress during a remodel is the chaos factor. You had to move the dishes, glasses, and silverware out of the cabinets, but where are they now?

To prevent lost-item stress, don't wait until the night before the installers show up to start clearing out the kitchen.

Although it may seem like extra work at the time, be sure to label all boxes with their contents as you move things out of the kitchen. This not only will save you hours when you're trying to locate items during the remodel period but will also make moving into your new kitchen that much easier. Keep the items you'll continue to use accessible and close by. Consider setting up a temporary pantry in the living room, dining room, or den. ▪

Finally, focus on the positive. And when all else fails, keep your sense of humor. Laughter truly is the best stress reliever of all.

MONEY

Okay, you understand the time factor and you can handle the stress. But what about the cost?

It's true that remodeling is a major expense, and like a new car, or the kids' college tuition, it will more than likely require a loan. People often have unrealistic expectations of what their remodeling dollars will buy, so make sure that your plans will fit into your budget.

Don't be fooled by TV shows that redo entire rooms for under $1,000. In the real world, the cost of remodeling your kitchen is akin to buying a new car. For a full remodel, you should plan to spend 10 to 20 percent of the value of your home. If you're just looking to spruce things up, you can do that less expensively. But even replacing the countertops and putting in a few new appliances will likely take a decent-sized chunk out of your bank account.

Later on, we'll look at budgeting and financing issues. But, before you try to decide how much you can or should spend, it's a good idea to do some research and get a sense of prices. After all, you wouldn't just pick a random amount of money and say, "I'm going to buy a car with this," would you? Nope, first you'd figure out what cars cost in general, what kind of car you want and what you can reasonably afford, and then figure out the best way to reconcile all of the above.

Get Ready to Poke and Pry: Why Thorough Research is a Must

So you've now reached the point where it's time to do some research. Except, your inner child wants to skip right over to the good part. After all, in college, you were the kind of person who started the paper the night before it was due, and that worked just fine. Why change things now, right?

Besides, you've seen home improvement shows on TV, and you've been in plenty of kitchens before. So why waste all that time doing research when you can just walk into a showroom and pick out what you like?

While this may sound like a great way to save time, it will actually cost you more time in the long run. Since kitchen remodeling requires a lot of choices, you need to educate yourself so you can make intelligent ones. Even if you're hiring a designer, the more you know up front, the less time you'll have to spend asking your designer questions. And since a designer's time costs *you* money, a little advance planning can save a lot of money. Advance research will also help you figure out what looks you really like, which can save you from getting railroaded into a look that's beautiful, but not really "you."

Remember, you're going to have to live with your product choices for many years to come. So, don't you think you should know the features, benefits, and advantages of each before handing over your hard-earned cash?

Finally, many products look alike, but vary widely when it comes to maintenance, durability, and warranties. An educated consumer is a consumer who doesn't get ripped off. So do your research, and don't be afraid to explore all the wonderful resources available—including a host of Web sites that offer free advice.

SURFING THE NET

Thanks to today's technology, you can begin doing your kitchen research without even leaving your house. Just turn on your computer and start to surf. Below are some great Web sites to help you research the kitchen design process.

www.nkba.org: The Web site of the National Kitchen & Bath Association lists the forty-one guidelines to kitchen design, links to member kitchen designers, lists of certified kitchen designers and certified master kitchen and bath designers, and a host of general information.

www.nari.org: The National Association of the Remodeling Industry is another good resource for researching all of your remodeling needs.

Kitchens.com is a great online research source with lots of free information about everything from products to budgeting. **PHOTO:** *Courtesy of Kitchens.com* ▼

www.Kitchens.com: This is a great place to find out nearly anything about kitchen design. The site offers everything from new products and design trends to color forecasts, budgeting tips, and links to area designers. You can even view actual kitchens done on a wide variety of budgets.

www.DIYOnline.com: For those looking to design their own kitchens, this Web site features tips, advice, and software from 20-20 Technologies that enables consumers to custom-design home-improvement projects according to their specifications.

www.handyman.com: For those looking to find a contractor, this Web site offers a list of prescreened candidates for everything from a full remodel to flooring installation to electrical rewiring. The site also boasts thousands of floor plans, discussion boards for do-it-yourselfers, and more.

Manufacturers' Web sites have become increasingly sophisticated, showing not only basic product photos, specs, and info, but also plenty of extras. On some, you can hit a single key to swap out finishes, change door styles, or see products in actual settings. It may not be the same as touching and seeing it live, but the online experience is getting more "real" every day.

Resources: Want to check out where the pros go? The following sites are geared for kitchen design professionals, but they also can provide interesting insights for the consumer looking to learn more about kitchen design:

www.kbdn.net

www.kitchenbathpros.com

www.qualifiedremodeler.com

WANT A KITCHEN STRAIGHT OUT OF A MAGAZINE?

Home and architectural magazines remain a great way to gather design information as well. You can even clip photos for future reference. Many will include source information—everything from floor plans to products used to designer credits. That way, if you find a look you like, you know exactly whom to contact for details.

Most likely, however, you'll start with magazines to get basic ideas, and then refine what you see to suit your individual needs. If you're working with a designer, you may want to start a file of design ideas so you can show your designer what you like. "See this built-in pantry with the pull-out shelves? I'd like something like this, only I have less space than this kitchen has. Is there a way to recess it into the wall? Or perhaps I can somehow use the dead corner space by the door to create storage and integrate it into the main kitchen?" Designers can help refine your magazine "dream file" to make it work for your own kitchen.

Other magazines such as *Family Handyman* offer practical advice for doing it yourself. Be warned, however, that if you can't hang a picture without cracking the wall in three places, a couple of back issues of a do-it-yourself magazine will not transform you into a one-man do-it-yourself band.

AS SEEN ON TV

When you've finished reading all those design magazines, turn on the TV. There's a proliferation of shows, from *Kitchen Design* to *Trading Spaces* to *Bob Vila* to *Surprise By Design,* offering design and do-it-yourself advice. These are a great way to start educating yourself about design styles and design lingo. They also offer helpful hints for the do-it-yourselfer.

Many of these shows will also help you visualize different kitchen layouts, see the benefits of each, and assist you in defining your own needs and preferences.

Be warned, however, that TV is not life. What you see between the commercials is still scripted and not necessarily reflective of real life. In real life, kitchens aren't about just looking good for the moment, they're about cooking, eating, and living in.

HOME CENTER, HOME SHOW

Web sites, magazines, and TV shows can certainly provide design inspiration, but nothing beats seeing products live. To view hundreds of products, all in one location, just let your feet do the walking through a Home EXPO, Lowe's, or other home design supercenter. Whether you're looking to browse or buy, a home center will give you plenty of ideas to

Remember that TV always includes an element of fantasy. For instance, that great room/kitchen layout you saw on TV may look big and inviting. But, before you decide this is your dream kitchen, think about whether this kind of space actually suits the way you live. In the house on TV, everything is neat and perfect. It's been professionally cleaned, the counters are clutter free, and there are no fingerprints or dirty dishes to mess things up. If your house tends to be more cluttered in real life, though, that great open space will mean your whole house will look messy if just a few things are out of place. Unless your life is a Hollywood vision, think real life as you plan your dream kitchen. ■

choose from. You can find everything from different edge treatments to walls and walls of cabinet doors.

Likewise, home shows can be a utopia for those looking for new design ideas. They offer the chance to see product displays as well as numerous kitchen vignettes or even full kitchens designed to showcase products as they might actually appear in your home. Check the home section of your local newspaper, or ask at a local home center or kitchen dealer.

While these shows are a great opportunity to see and touch a wide array of products and

A show house is a great place to see cutting-edge designs from top designers. **DESIGNER:** *Jamie Gibbs, ASID, IFDA, Jamie Gibbs and Associates, in conjunction with Roberta Bauer-Kravette, ASID Trade Partner, Nieuw Amsterdam Kitchens—A Division of Transitions Kitchens and Interiors, Inc.* ◀

design styles, they also offer a chance to talk to many people "in the biz." That means you get to comparison shop and make contacts with designers, installers, and other industry pros.

Many home shows also include free seminars to help educate you about everything from product selection to financing options.

SHOW HOUSE, OPEN HOUSE

Of course, if you want to see the latest, greatest thing in design in an actual home, show houses are a great way to go. They not only feature the work of some of the biggest design names in the industry, they also support local charitable organizations. So in doing your research, you can also rack up good karma points.

Show house kitchens are just what the name implies. They are houses designed to show off the work of the designer. Since the emphasis is on the "show," most tend toward the showy. That means you'll see designs that spotlight the unusual, exotic, dramatic, or spectacular. These are not your basic white kitchens—so don't be surprised if you see cobalt blue appliances, zebra-wood countertops, hand-painted imported tile murals, or poured and stained concrete floors.

It's all about cutting-edge design, so if your own taste leans more toward the "safe side," these may not be up your alley. However, show houses are a great place to see what's new, while previewing the work of area designers. Even if you're not that daring, you may find one detail you'd like to incorporate and personalize on a smaller scale in your own kitchen design.

Sometimes, kitchen dealers and local organizations also sponsor house tours or open houses, where you can see a variety of newly designed kitchens in your area. These tend to be more real-life kitchens, since they were designed for ordinary people like you.

What's so exciting about getting a peek at someone else's kitchen? Oh, come on! It's legalized snooping, and what can be better than that? After all, what better way to see how the Joneses live—all under the socially acceptable guise of "research"?

But whether you prefer to do your research live, on the Net, or through books, magazines, and TV, try to see as many kitchens (and kitchen products) as possible. Before you know it, you'll be able to explain exactly what your dream kitchen will look like! Now, you just need to decide the best way to bring that dream to life.

Hire a Pro, Do It Yourself, or Buy It Yourself?

The first thing to ask yourself is, do you really need to hire a professional kitchen designer? Or do you have the time and skills to handle this project solo? Is shopping your favorite pastime, and if so, can you buy your own prod- ucts and just get help on the installation side? Or will two-hundred-plus choices of countertop patterns send you screaming into the night?

If you don't know which way to go, take this short quiz:

1. *Granite is your top pick for countertops because:*
   A. A dark green honed surface will coor- dinate well with the Shaker-style cabi- netry and stainless-steel appliances you have planned for the rest of the space.
   B. *Family Handyman Magazine* had a great article on how to install it your- self, and you know a guy who works for a fabricator.
   C. Home EXPO is having a sale, so you can afford it!
   D. It looks pretty in your next-door neighbor's house.

2. *When it comes to your handyman abilities:*
   A. You've done it all—plumbing, electri- cal, and carpentry. In fact, you did such a good job building the deck out back (with retractable sunroof and built-in BBQ, refrigerator, and multilevel heat- ing), Home Depot has called YOU asking if you'd be interested in a job.
   B. You've handled several moderate-sized home repair projects, and are confident in your abilities, but you draw the line at

certain projects. For instance, you won't handle complicated electrical work because you know a house fire would mean you'd have to redo *everything,* not just one room.
   C. You can handle some basic fix-it stuff, but you prefer to leave the complicated stuff to the pros.
   D. You once nearly electrocuted yourself screwing in a light bulb.

3. *Your regular work schedule is:*
   A. Work? You mean, like, an actual job? But if you had a day job, who would play with the dog?
   B. Part time.
   C. Nine to five, but with some flexibility.
   D. Days, nights, weekends, holidays . . . if you spent any more time there, they'd start charging you rent.

4. *You view shopping as:*
   A. Something you excel at. You have an excellent sense of style; Chris Madden has nothing on you!
   B. The holy grail—you once spent a month searching out the perfect shower curtain to pick up the silver-blue trim on the custom mirror you found at a lit- tle boutique miles off the beaten track.
   C. You're okay if you know in advance what you're looking for, but just brows- ing around bores you to tears.

D. You only go to stores that have couches and TV sets—and even then, you have to be dragged kicking and screaming.

If you answered all As, you probably have the time, knowledge, and ability to go solo. Mostly Bs may make you a good candidate for buy-it-yourself (then hire someone to handle the hard stuff). Cs and Ds suggest you might want to hire a professional.

So Many Options, So Little Time

When it comes to kitchen shopping, there are options galore. You can choose a traditional kitchen showroom, an independent designer, a home center, or the do-it-yourself route. Each of these has advantages and disadvantages, depending on your needs and budget. Here's the lowdown on each:

OPTION	THE BIG ADVANTAGE	THE DOWN SIDE
The Traditional Kitchen Showroom	You can view a host of displays, including many complete kitchens and kitchen vignettes that will help give you an idea of what your kitchen will look like *before* it's a permanent part of your house. One-stop shopping, and top-grade personal service also help to minimize stress and give you a go-to person when problems crop up.	You are paying for those advantages.
The Independent Designer	Because they don't have a showroom, there's less overhead, and those savings can be passed on to you. They also tend to be known for their cutting-edge designs and creative approach.	You may have to monitor your own installation and buy your own appliances. There's also no showroom for you to preview different styles, or see how those pink-toned maple cabinets look in a complete kitchen setting.
The Home Center Plus Installer	Home centers buy in bulk, and therefore generally get cheaper prices that can translate to big savings for you. There's a huge array of products on display, so you'll have a wide selection to choose from. You can also get everything from installers to electrical and plumbing help through most home centers.	Design resources are either up to you, or done by an in-house designer who is frequently time strapped and overworked. As a result, designs tend to be of the cookie-cutter variety. A large retail store environment may mean personal service is less personal than you'd like, and installation can be complicated, since this work is contracted out.

OPTION	THE BIG ADVANTAGE	THE DOWN SIDE
Get Out the Hammer and Drill	You get maximum bang for your buck.	If you're not an experienced and capable Mr. or Ms. Fix-it, this approach has the potential for maximum disaster (think *Trading Spaces* without the designer).

THE TRADITIONAL KITCHEN SHOWROOM

If you're looking for a place where you can talk to expert kitchen designers, see products in actual kitchen settings, and get knowledgeable help with everything from picking out a color scheme to figuring out what appliances best suit your cooking skills, the kitchen showroom is the place for you. It is staffed by kitchen design professionals and offers a plethora of choices, so you can see, touch, and experience the products before you sign that check.

Many even have working appliances that you can test-drive before you buy, so you can actually cook on that great-looking Dacor range before committing to it.

Working through a kitchen showroom can also minimize your stress level. You can deal with a professional who not only designs kitchens, but who can also anticipate problems and help you prepare for the process. Since kitchen dealers specialize in personalized service, they can knowledgeably guide you through a process that can seem overwhelming at times, due to the endless number of choices. They can

create a design that works for you, help you pick out products best geared for your specific needs (and explain the differences between these products), work with you to set up a budget, and even help you secure financing.

Kitchen dealers can also give you a complete price—including the design, products, installation, and plenty of hand-holding along the way—so there's less guesswork involved.

The best kitchens are installed with care and an eye for detail. DESIGNER: *John Sofio (Built, Inc.)* ◀

THE INDEPENDENT DESIGNER

Independent designers are highly trained design professionals who focus their talents exclusively on design, rather than splitting their focus on the runnings of a showroom. They specialize in personalizing kitchens, so if you're looking for an unusual or one-of-a-kind kitchen, this may be the way to go.

Generally, they will come to your home, look at your kitchen, listen to your needs, and design a kitchen around those needs. Your designer may also accompany you to other retail outlets to show you products, give product advice, facilitate product ordering, and suggest installers.

While a good independent designer will help facilitate the entire process from conception to completion—and may even recommend an installer—you will still have to deal with more people than if you went with a full turnkey operation. For instance, you will likely have a separate contract with the installer. That means if things go wrong on that end, you will have to deal with the installer directly.

THE HOME CENTER PLUS INSTALLER

Home centers offer some of the best prices around. Since they can afford to buy in large quantities, they are able to pass those savings on to their customers. And, because of their size, many offer a huge array of product choices. There's plenty to see at a home center, and it's a great place to start your research, even if you're not planning on ultimately buying there.

Many home centers offer everything from product and design to installation, plumbing, and electrical services.

For those who are somewhat handy, several of the home center chains regularly offer seminars to help people refine their DIY skills. Even if you're not ready to do it yourself, these are a good way to educate yourself about the basics. ■

Free computerized design services, available at many home centers, also add to home centers' appeal. These allow you to walk out with a computer-drawn kitchen plan that you can then show to family and friends before making a commitment.

However, if you're looking for serious

A home entertainment center is now often part of the new millennium great room.
PHOTO: *Courtesy of Canyon Creek* ◀

hand-holding, you may find a home center a bit too big, and busy, to suit your needs. Because they service a huge volume of clients, they rarely provide the kind of personalized service you can get from a smaller kitchen dealership. That atmosphere may also be less relaxing, as you know if you've ever been lost in aisle eighteen, trying to identify a faucet that appears to be thirty feet off the ground, while simultaneously avoiding the guy trying to run you over with the beeping cart.

GET OUT THAT HAMMER AND DRILL!

If you have the time, skills, and equipment, you can save thousands of dollars going the do-it-yourself route. If you've been installing floors since you and your dad bonded over retiling Mom's new kitchen at age nine, it makes no sense to pay hundreds of dollars to some other guy. Installing a new kitchen requires knowl-edge, skill, experience, and proper equipment, but it's not brain surgery, either—although sometimes it seems to cost as much when you have to pay for installation.

So, if you've got what it takes—and trust us, part of what it takes is experience, because your new kitchen is *not* the place to decide to learn new skills—you can save a lot of money and get personal satisfaction from a job well done.

Just don't be fooled by what you see on TV, where beautiful rooms are designed and installed perfectly in thirty minutes or less by rank beginners. TV isn't real life, and they don't show you the outtakes. That means you never see the episode where the floor ends up slanted downward so steeply the dog's dish has to be mounted to the ground with steel brackets to keep it from sliding away. Don't bite off more than you can chew—and if you feel out of your depth during the project, don't be afraid to call for help.

Finally, recognize that anything that can set off fires, floods, or natural disasters should be left to the professionals. "Knowing something about electrical" is *not* the same as being an electrician, and no amount of money saved can make up for waking up one night to find your house on fire.

Measuring and Drawing Up a Plan

Now that you know what you want to do with your kitchen, and who you're going to have install it, you need to take measurements. If

If you're planning on expanding the existing footprint of the kitchen by either "pushing out" or "borrowing" space from another room, consider bringing in a professional. Permits may be necessary in order to make structural changes. Likewise, issues such as the placement of load-bearing walls can impact your ability to expand the kitchen. ■

you're keeping the same layout and merely changing out existing cabinets, countertops, or appliances with same-size replacements, your task is relatively easy. Just measure the items you are replacing. Do this twice to play it safe.

In the case of free-standing appliances, you'll also want to measure the space where the appliance is located. That way, if you fall in love with a refrigerator that's two inches wider than your existing one, you'll know if you have space for it. Remember, certain appliances have mandated clearances, so don't just assume that the extra inch you have between the range and the sink is usable space. Check with a professional first.

Once you have all your measurements, you're ready to head to your local home center or kitchen dealership and start looking at products.

If you're planning to change the layout, or expand or reconfigure cabinets or countertop space, however, the process gets a bit more complicated.

First, you'll need to carefully measure your entire kitchen. Draw a picture of the space, writing out the dimensions of each wall. You need to measure both width and height. All dimensions should be written out in inches.

Next, mark the drawing to note where any windows and doors are, as well as any pipes, plumbing, or radiators that you either can't move or don't want to move. Measure windows and doors for both height and width.

When measuring doors and windows, measure from the outside of the trim on one side to the outside of the trim on the other side. The trim is considered part of the door or window. ■

For radiators, plumbing, pipes, or other occlusions, you need to measure not only the height and width, but also how many inches they protrude from the wall.

Finally, measure where these are in relation to the end of the wall, floor, and ceiling. Draw these into your floor plan, marking the dimensions of each.

Sample Drawing

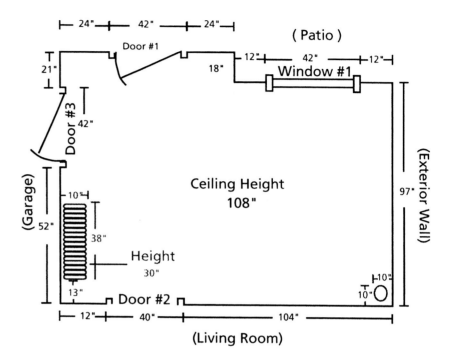

Design Software

Once you have the measurements, you have several options. If you're computer savvy, you can download or purchase one of the various kitchen design software programs created specifically for consumers.

Just Google "kitchen design software" and you'll get tons of hits, with many programs available for about the same price as "1,001 Fun Games of Solitaire for Windows." Some can even be yours for a thirty-day free trial. This software can be a great tool to help conceptualize your ideas. Even if you ultimately hire a professional designer, your ideas will be more organized and coherent than if you just jotted them down on a legal pad.

Before you head off to a kitchen designer or home center, draw a rough floor plan and write in measurements, noting the placement of windows, doors, radiators, pipes, etc. SOURCE: *Kitchens.com* ◀

The software programs require that you enter the dimensions of your kitchen, and any existing cabinetry, appliances, etc. that you are planning on leaving in place. The program will then allow you to try out a variety of layouts, while incorporating different kitchen products.

WARNING: While DIY software is inexpensive, kitchen design software for the professional market has a four-to-five figure price tag, and many professional designers find it difficult to learn. This is a hint. Getting your ideas together in a drawing is one thing. Developing a blueprint from which you will actually be ordering and purchasing expensive kitchen products of specific dimensions is quite another. Be honest with yourself about your skill level here, tech heads. You don't want to find yourself three months later with a four-inch gap between your countertop and wall, or a cabinet whose door won't open because of the way it's positioned next to the refrigerator.

Once you choose a working layout, you'll be able to see approximately how many linear feet of cabinets and countertops you'll need. Then you can start pricing products.

If, on the other hand, you'd prefer to leave the computer stuff to someone else, bring your room measurements to a home center or kitchen dealer. Tell them what you want to change or add. Many home centers will provide you with free computerized drawings of several possible kitchen layouts.

Likewise, many kitchen dealers will provide computerized drawings or even hand-drawn renderings to help you visualize a variety of kitchen possibilities.

The drawings you get from a professional kitchen designer tend to be more detailed and complex than those you would get elsewhere. They often offer highly personalized design solutions rather than a few standard cookie-cutter kitchen layouts. As a result, kitchen dealers often charge a design fee for these. However, the majority will apply that fee to the cost of your project if you hire their firm to handle your kitchen. ■

Your working layout will give you a better idea of what options are available to you. With your plan in hand, and the design ideas you picked up from all your research, you're ready to take the next step in the planning process: finding a design style that works for you.

CHAPTER 4

FINDING YOUR DESIGN STYLE

There are a million design styles out there these days. Some have multiple names, and some are grouped together under one big umbrella, such as Traditional.

Be careful. They don't have any truth in packaging laws for design, and some salespeople will tell you anything. For instance, they'll try to convince you that you can have a huge contemporary stainless-steel refrigerator next to ornate Old World cabinets with extra carvings and two kinds of glaze (all of which will cost extra), and it will look fine. Eclectic is how they might describe this, while trying to keep a straight face.

Well, guess what? Somewhere out there, there is a brilliant professional designer who could indeed make that combo look great. That brilliant professional designer has extensive cre-

dentials and probably some certifications, plus he or she studied architectural history in college and knows volumes more about design than you do. If *you* put those frilly cabinets next to that monster-truck fridge, however, it's going to look awful. (And truth be told, we've seen some professionally designed "eclectic" kitchens that are pretty darn hideous, too.)

If you're going to create your own design with the help of a home center, do yourself a favor—*keep it simple*. Pick a design theme and stick to it. And don't forget to think about the function requirements discussed in Chapter 2.

Here is a rundown of basic design styles and their subgenres.

Contemporary

Think of a cool loft in New York or Tokyo. Contemporary looks are sleek and streamlined, frequently incorporating striking geometric shapes and a hip, edgy feel.

European Contemporary is a more upscale, glossy look than its more casual American counterpart, variously referred to as Urban Industrial or Loft. European manufacturers do an amazing job with this style, but it's expensive. For instance, a kitchen built around Gaggenau's stunning line of ultramodern aluminum appliances will cost you *way* far into five figures.

Keep in mind, too, that clutter looks a lot worse in a kitchen that's all cold, clean lines than it does in a softer look with collectibles on display. So if you have a bustling, slightly messy kind of kitchen, it's going to be hard to maintain a minimalist look in the pristine shape it deserves.

If you have the budget and organizational skills to pull off European Contemporary, hire a professional designer who has extensive relationships with European manufacturers.

Pacific Rim is an Asian-inspired take on Soft Contemporary that presents a beautifully subtle, carefully planned, serene environment replete with natural materials and a sense of balance. Look to traditional Japanese design elements such as shoji screens for cues. Pacific Rim design is more complex than it looks, and generally requires a designer who's knowledgeable about feng shui and other Asian design principles.

Soft Contemporary: One hundred years from now, when people are doing new millennium style as a vintage design, they'll be doing Soft Contemporary. If you want to do a classy, elegant look that's not overdecorated or gimmicky, this is the perfect choice.

Soft Contemporary espouses clean lines, but not hard lines, paired with neutral, soothing colors. Its style elements derive from interesting textures and shapes, such as satin and brushed finishes on metal, subdued tone-on-tone countertop colors, and simple, sleek cabinets that show the beauty of the wood.

European minimalist looks are beautiful but pricey and are best suited only for the neat and organized. PHOTO: *Courtesy of Gaggenau* ◀

A simple finish on your cabinetry is perfect for a Soft Contemporary look. Here, a Sonoma Cast Stone concrete countertop enhances a serene, clean-lined feel. PHOTO: *Courtesy of Sonoma Cast Stone* ▶

When doing a Soft Contemporary look, you can let function dictate form. Start by picking the appliances and countertop material that will work best for your family, in terms of function and budget. You're not limited by basic design truths such as, they didn't have solid surface in the court of Louis XV. You have solid surface today, and you're doing today's look.

Urban Industrial, otherwise known as Loft, takes its cues from the factory, and is a cutting-edge, up-and-coming look. A utilitarian, unadorned vibe is what you're after here. For Urban Industrial, function rules! For instance, an undermount steel sink paired with a practical faucet such as a polished chrome pull-out would be perfect.

Especially if you have a limited budget, look at materials meant for restaurant, industrial, and factory use—they'll add both character and a unique look to your kitchen. For instance, one of those giant metal some-assembly-required shelves across one wall will give you a whole lot of storage and the look of stainless steel. Or how about those textured rubber squares they use in warehouses for flooring? Plain black vinyl tile is another low-cost option. Or add an interesting texture with plain gray slate. For countertops, engineered stone such as CaesarStone's honed Concrete is a great pick for an Urban Industrial look.

STYLE ALERT: The Whirlpool Gladiator GarageWorks series features affordable storage

cabinets and appliances designed for the garage. But their rugged, stylish, diamondback metal look would make for a terrific addition to an Urban Industrial kitchen as well. Check 'em out at www.gladiatorgw.com.

RESOURCES: *Dwell* and *Metropolitan Home* magazines are both fans of the Loft look, and will have many ideas for you.

Transitional

Think of an old silent movie star's home or Frank Lloyd Wright. Twentieth-century design comes in many forms, from glamorous Art Deco,

to simple, clean-lined Arts & Crafts styles, to quirky, hip Modern Retro (aka Mid-century Modern). Transitional is more warm and homey than most contemporary looks, but more streamlined than traditional. Transitional looks are now rapidly gaining in popularity, so this is a good category to consider if resale value is an issue.

Art Deco gets its name from the 1925 Exposition Internationale des Arts Décoratifs Industriels et Modernes in Paris. The exposition celebrated living in the modern world, and so does Deco. It brought a modern spin to antique Greek, Roman, Egyptian, Mayan, and other old design styles, and coupled these with modern elements.

Art Deco is a beautifully sophisticated, upscale look that includes the use of exotic

The Gladiator GarageWorks series is designed for the garage, but would work well for an Urban Industrial kitchen as well. **PHOTO:** *Courtesy of Gladiator* ▲

woods and veneers on lacquered, luxurious furniture. A professional designer or extensive research and a major-league sense of style are musts if you want an Art Deco kitchen. The same goes for Art Nouveau, an earlier (late 1800s/early 1900s) but somewhat similar movement in art, design, and architecture.

RESOURCES: www.decopix.com, www.art-deco.org

Arts & Crafts design has a traditional, warm feel that's paired with clean, modern, geometric lines—nothing the least bit fussy or cutesy.

Arts & Crafts started in England as a rebel movement against mass production and the Industrial Revolution. The heyday of Arts & Crafts was 1890–1930. This design trend is also referred to as Craftsman, Mission, California Bungalow, and American Bungalow.

Transitional looks are rapidly gaining in popularity, making them a good design choice when thinking of resale value. DESIGNER: *Ulrich, Inc.* PHOTO: *David Van Scott* ▼

The purveyors of Arts & Crafts style were really ahead of their time, and espoused the principles that many design/build firms hold today: a rapport between architect, designer, and craftsman in designing stylish and affordable housing. Arts & Crafts designers also used an open floor plan and a lot of built-ins. They favored wood and other natural materials for a look that's cheerful, durable, and meant to be lived in.

RESOURCES: Gustav Stickley, one of the Arts & Crafts movement's bright lights, had a furniture line

Modern Retro features a modern but quirky look.
DESIGNER: *Ellen Cheever, CMKBD, ASID (Ellen Cheever and Associates)* ◀

in his time. Today, his heirs are still at it (www. stickley.com). Restoration Hardware (www. restorationhardware.com) also has beautiful, authentic-looking furniture for an Arts & Crafts kitchen/great room; www.crafthome.com has links to all things Arts & Crafts, from clocks to copper range hoods. See also www.arts-crafts.com for more information on this design style.

Modern Retro: You know how 1950s movies about the space age tried to predict what things were going to look like in the future? But their futuristic year 2000 wasn't quite what the real 2000 was like. Welcome to

The Arts & Crafts period produced a lot of decorative items such as vases and geometric stained-glass pieces. These little add-ons can do a lot to give your kitchen an authentic period feel without spending a huge amount of money. ■

the world of Modern Retro. This is a look where contemporary and vintage clash in a really great way, giving us Danish Modern

A metal edge lends this solid surface countertop a retro feel.
PHOTO: *Courtesy of Laminations Unlimited and Barry Tupis* ▶

chairs, the furniture villains had in early James Bond movies, or in Vegas, circa the Rat Pack—modern, but quirky.

Modern Retro is now a huge, cutting-edge design trend that is bound to get more mainstream. So if you're a cool, forward-thinking kind of person, this is a good bet for your kitchen.

If you're doing a great room that includes a family home entertainment area, you have a lot of choices in Modern Retro furniture, both vintage and stylish reproductions. Many faucet lines now also feature retro looks in classic polished chrome or its updated cousin, polished nickel. For a classy Danish Modern feel, frameless slab doors in a natural wood tone are a perfect cabinet choice. For more of a 1950s *Leave It to Beaver* vibe, try a white painted door paired with hardware that has a retro look.

RESOURCES: www.retromodern.com, www.gomod.com, www.velocityartanddesign.com, www.nova68.com. A case study of a young couple who accomplished their retro kitchen remodel is presented at retroplanet.net/2kitchen.html.

Traditional

One of those buzzwords that kitchen dealers throw around, "traditional" usually means "anything that doesn't look contemporary." Emotionally, Traditional styling has a pillar-of-the-community vibe. The White House is decorated in Traditional. Colonial Williamsburg is Traditional, imbued with a solid, conservative feel that stands the test of time.

Just like that Burberry trenchcoat, a string of pearls, or Levi's 501s, a Traditional kitchen will never seem ridiculous when you look at the photos twenty years from now. But here's why this style is trickier than it looks:

Technically, what people mean when they say Traditional is American seventeeth- to late nineteenth-century design. But just like with Old World, there are many, many styles that get lumped into Traditional. Do you know the difference between Federal and Georgian style? How about Cape Cod versus Dutch Colonial?

Again, this is where professional designers who know their stuff can really help you out. And that kid at the home center who got transferred from the tool corral to the kitchen section last week does not qualify as a professional designer. Don't just throw in a mishmash of crown molding and raised panel fronts and think you have Traditional. If you do this look badly, it will look cluttered and stuffy.

You'll also have to deal with the matter of anachronistic appliances and countertop materials. They did not have speed-cooking ovens, temperature-controlled wine coolers, and undermount sinks during the Civil War, and mixing these modern products with cabinet styles that were around when Sherman was

A traditional look, done right, has a timeless, solid feel that never goes out of style. DESIGNER: *Gail Drury, CKD/ CBD (Drury Designs)* PHOTO: *Kristine Wolff, Kristine Wolff Photography*

burning Atlanta usually takes the expertise of a professional designer.

If you're remodeling an older house, investigate its history, and then think about some design cues you can derive from that.

RESOURCES: Kitchens.com has a great section that analyzes architectural styles and makes suggestions for a compatible kitchen. See also www.traditionalhome.com.

Even if you're putting a Traditional kitchen into a brand-new suburban ranch home, you can still look at the history of Traditional style. Design has meaning; people made things the way they did for a reason. So, go into a remodel knowing where historical elements came from, and why they are meaningful to you. Make sure your Traditional design has a real sense of tradition.

Old World

Another umbrella definition encompassing many periods and styles from different countries, Old World design evokes the Europe of centuries past. It features lots of ornate, intricate design flourishes and luxurious materials.

Please do not try to do Old World if you don't have a generous budget ($50,000 plus). There's nothing tackier than that "Kmart antique" vibe. Classic Old World styling is all

about intricate carvings and beaded insets, architectural details, and beautiful stone surfaces.

If you're going to do Old World, do it right. Get a professional designer who knows the difference between, say, Renaissance French antiques and Louis XV French antiques. And as with American Traditional, educate yourself. Go to a museum and look at the displays of

Old World styles feature ornate, intricate flourishes and an antique, luxurious look. PHOTO: *Courtesy of White River Hardwoods-Woodworks, Inc.* ▲

antique furnishings. Take an architectural history class at your local college. Learn to differentiate between periods and styles. Don't end up with some of the unfortunate subsets you see so often, such as "Sopranos Wannabe Italian Baroque" and "Looks Fancy, Must Be Good French Provincial."

RESOURCES: Here are a couple of sites to get you started: www.antiques-finder.co.uk, and www.faccents.com.

Country French or Rustic Tuscany looks can be beautiful— when done by a professional designer. This kitchen features a charming wood checkerboard by Craft-Art Countertops.

PHOTO: *Courtesy of The Craft-Art Company, Inc.* ▼

Country French and **Rustic Tuscany** are a sometimes charming, sometimes unfortunate mix of Rustic, Country, Mediterranean, and Old World looks. The problem with these styles is, it's very easy to degenerate into frilly clutter, the design equivalent of those horrible haircuts people sometimes impose upon their poodles, who surely walk around thinking, "I'm a nice dog, why do I have silly pink bows in my fur?" More truly ghastly kitchens come from European Country looks gone wrong than anything else.

Mediterranean and **Spanish Colonial** style lends itself to warm climates, and indeed, these looks are extremely popular in Southern California, Florida, and Texas. Mediterranean done well is luxurious, relaxed, and beautiful. If done badly, you get "Valley-Girl Mediterranean," the pastel concoction favored by some misguided Los Angeles condo architects. Mediterranean is usually ruined by making it too frilly, as opposed to sticking to classic Spanish Colonial styling,

Tip

Many areas that have Mediterranean and Art Deco architecture have some sort of historical organization that organizes tours of classic houses. If you are a fan of these design styles, a tour will give you a wealth of beautiful, historically accurate ideas. ■

or the Art Deco-laced California stucco designs of the 1920s.

Overall, Mediterranean style is marked by a lot of tile, terra cotta and stone flooring, ornate wrought-iron hardware, white walls with dark, rich woods, and interesting curved architectural details on windows and doorways. Hand-painted ceramic tile is another hallmark of Mediterranean style.

RESOURCES: www.stpete.org/Mediterranean.htm, www.architect.com/Publish/Trad_Build.html

Country

Think of your grandma's or great-grandma's kitchen. A country kitchen has a relaxed, warm feeling. It's down-home, inviting, and friendly. A Country look can spotlight authentic vintage collectibles, which always makes for a more individual design statement.

Start with real pieces that are your heirlooms, or someone else's. Here's where you can really benefit from actually going out to the country. Don't go for pseudocountry plastic junk from the mall. Take a weekend trip out to the boonies, visit that charming crafts and collectibles store, and discover the items you want to collect.

For instance, Depression glass is really beautiful. Or consider old fruit box labels that

Country looks frequently make a design statement with authentic collectibles. Here, a high-end antique version. DESIGNER: *Julie Stoner, CKD, ASID (Rutt Studio on the Main Line)* ◀

you can frame. Displays of old china, vintage tablecloths from the 1940s, or old bread boxes are also great. Functionality is big in Country design—a country kitchen is a hard-working kitchen—so a wrought-iron rack with hanging copper-bottom pots is a nice touch. The white fire clay or vitreous china farmer sink makes a great centerpiece for your Country kitchen.

RESOURCES: For lots of authentic-looking vintage sinks, see www.vintagetub.com.

For flooring, consider good old checkerboard linoleum, perhaps in a quieter color scheme than black and white. How about a grayish blue and white Marmoleum checkerboard to go with the blue tones in that faded vintage-print tablecloth that you're going to have made into curtains? A Country look is a little worn around the edges.

STYLE ALERT: When doing Country, take it easy on the cute stuff. Cute can easily cross the line into icky-cutesy if you're not careful. So, while Country style can definitely involve patterns featuring chickens, cows and other farm animals, as well as things that are flowered, quilted, or feminine—less is more with the adorable baby goats and lace doilies.

RESOURCES: http://countryjoe.bizland.com/ctry-1.html, www.greatwindsorchairs.com, www.countrycritter.com, many more

Shabby Chic offers a more ethereal, romantic, Victorian version of a country look, with more antique-y thrift shop finds, more wicker, and more white. Shabby Chic is all about artful clutter, for instance, a collection of vintage colored-glass bottles on the windowsill.

RESOURCES: There are many informative Web sites and books, primarily by Rachel Ashwell, available about this design style.

Rustic/Southwest

Think of a ranch in New Mexico or a log cabin in Colorado, replete with wood, stone, and other natural materials. There may be a folk art influence, with distressing for a well-worn look.

This is a comfortable, homey style, but more rugged than Country. Rustic is a guy's kind of kitchen, where you might be preparing venison, or your grandpa's famous chili recipe. Hickory is a fine cabinet choice for your Rustic kitchen. For the color scheme, think of the desert and mountains: cactus green, Grand Canyon rock colors, combined with the bright color combinations in a Native American blanket.

RESOURCES: www.elantiquario.com, www.cowboy.com

Hickory cabinetry is a great choice for a Rustic look. PHOTO: *Courtesy of KraftMaid* ◀

Ethnic, Folk Art–Inspired looks are a great way of giving your kitchen a theme. Pick your own heritage—or just one you've always had an affinity for—and do some research. Think of what kind of look your home's overall architecture lends itself to. Spanish? African? Asian? Hawaiian? Use your imagination.

Look at traditional design elements and think of new ways to apply them. For instance, there was a great *Trading Spaces* kitchen that used broken Mexican pottery pieces as a mosaic backsplash. The space also featured perforated metal appliqués on the cabinet doors, yellow walls, and a colorful blanket-style throw rug.

Eclectic

Another major buzz word these days, "Eclectic" mostly means, throw a bunch of styles together and call it "putting a new spin on old looks." Eclectic can be brilliant if done by a great designer, and just hideous otherwise. Like they say when hauling *Fear Factor* contestants up by pulleys fifty feet above a convoy of monster trucks, "Don't try this at home." Have a point of view to your design.

A Look at Design Styles by Budget

Some design styles lend themselves to a tight budget, and a DIY approach, while others don't. In large part, it depends on where the design originated. For instance, if a style was meant for the royalty of a particular era, it's going to be much, much harder to reproduce yourself for a low-end budget than a design that was originally created by farmers. Complex, high-end looks also make the services of a professional designer a must.

But, but, you say, "I love antiques! I've always loved antiques, I don't want a contemporary kitchen!" And you don't have to get one. You can design a fine Shabby Chic or Country kitchen on a low budget, because with those styles, the focal point will be displayed collectibles, not the actual kitchen cabinetry. These themes also have a worn, faded, down-home feel, so it's possible to find salvage and flea-market furniture pieces and refurbish them to give your kitchen the style without the price tag.

We've included this handy chart to better explain which styles work with a limited budget, and which do not. See Chapter 6, "Design on a Shoestring," for more tips on how to get the look you want for less.

In the following chart, note that the styles cited under "Micro to Low" budget can also be done on the high end. For instance, you can certainly have a Modern Retro kitchen/great room which incorporates original Eames furniture that retails for five figures. But these styles will also lend themselves to a limited budget, while those in the shaded areas do not.

DESIGN STYLE	HIGH TO ULTRA HIGH ($40K–$75K+)	LOW TO MID ($15K–$40K)	MICRO TO LOW ($1K–$15K)
CONTEMPORARY (New Millennium Design) THINK: a cool loft in NYC, sleek, cutting edge, minimalist, streamlined, uncluttered KEY PRODUCTS: Stainless-steel appliances, undermount sinks, engineered stone, solid surface, brushed hardware finishes	European Contemporary	Soft Contemporary Pacific Rim	Urban Industrial aka Loft

DESIGN STYLE	HIGH TO ULTRA HIGH ($40K–$75K+)	LOW TO MID ($15K–$40K)	MICRO TO LOW ($1K–$15K)
TRANSITIONAL (Twentieth-century design) THINK: Frank Lloyd Wright, decor in old movies, Modernist influence, quirky, a clean-lined look that still has a retro, vintage feel KEY PRODUCTS: Shaker cabinets, linoleum, polished chrome, copper, stone, and tile	Art Deco, Art Nouveau	Arts & Crafts aka Mission	Modern Retro aka Mid-century Modern
TRADITIONAL (Formal pre-twentieth-century American) THINK: White House, Colonial Williamsburg, solid, conservative KEY PRODUCTS: raised-panel cabinetry	American Colonial, Georgian, Federal, Cape Cod, more		Shabby Chic
OLD WORLD (Formal pre-twentieth-century European) THINK: a palace in Europe, ornate, luxurious, architectural details KEY PRODUCTS: carved inlays, glossy stone, oil-rubbed bronze finish	Queen Anne, Tudor, Rococo, French Provincial, Gothic, Elizabethan, Victorian, more	Spanish Colonial, Mediterranean Revival	Shabby Chic
COUNTRY (Informal, inspired by rural design) THINK: your grandma's kitchen, down-home, warm, artful clutter, lived-in, faded KEY PRODUCTS: white farmer sink, wall-mounted faucets, butcher block	French Country, Rustic Tuscany		American Country

DESIGN STYLE	HIGH TO ULTRA HIGH ($40K–$75K+)	LOW TO MID ($15K–$40K)	MICRO TO LOW ($1K–$15K)
RUSTIC/REGIONAL/WORLD (Inspired by world, regional, ethnic design) THINK: Colorado cabin, rugged, comfortable, Santa Fe stucco house, cactus, Grand Canyon, Native American blanket colors KEY PRODUCTS: hickory cabinetry, brick, wrought iron, ceramic tile		Rustic/Southwest	Folk Art/Ethnic–inspired Design

Shaded areas equal don't try this by yourself. These looks need the help of a professional designer as well as a generous or at least substantial mid-range budget.

Hopefully, at least one of these styles resonates with you. Now that you understand a bit more about design styles, it's time to take a look at color, and how it impacts your kitchen design.

In Living Color

Most people know that dark or bright colors will make a room feel smaller, while softer, lighter, more neutral colors will make a room feel larger. But color can do a lot more than that. Effective use of color can draw attention away from imperfections, visually lower or raise a ceiling, shorten or lengthen a room, or even make you feel relaxed, revved up, hungry, or tired.

Do you hate your kitchen's size or shape as much as you hate those ten pounds you can never quite diet away? Clever use of color isn't just for fashion. The same principles can be used to fool the eye so that it visually changes the dimensions of your kitchen. For instance, if you want to create the illusion of a lower ceiling, warm colors and dark tones will do the trick, while cool colors and lighter tints can make a ceiling seem higher. Likewise, a long room can be made to seem shorter with warm or darker colors, while a short room can be made to appear longer with cool, light colors.

COLOR AND YOUR SENSES

While we perceive color visually, it actually affects all of the senses. Studies show that the color red enhances the effects of sweet smells, while shades of blue or green reduce them. Orange helps makes us more sensitive to peppery or spicy scents, while cool or warm colors actually tend to make us feel either colder, or warmer.

Perception of time is also influenced by colors. Soft, relaxing blues seem to slow time down, while bright colors speed it up. (This is why so many casinos are done in shades of red.) Color can also create a sense of heaviness or weight: a dark-colored object seems physically heavier or denser, while lighter colors have the opposite effect. Consequently, smaller kitchens tend to work best if large items, such as that bulky refrigerator, are light colored.

Does your kitchen have one feature you hate but can't get rid of, such as an ugly support beam or sloped ceiling area? Surround the area with a bright splash of color, or several contrasting colors. It will call attention away from the flaw. ■

COLOR AND MOOD

Remember the mood rings of the 1970s that promised to tell your mood by the color the ring turned when you put it on? While mood rings were a passing fad, the relationship between color and mood is not.

Studies have shown that color not only

creates an ambiance, it impacts your mood, appetite, and even blood pressure.

So, when you're picking color choices, think about what effect you want—calming, stimulating, elegant, or casual—and choose your color scheme accordingly.

THE 60–30–10 SPLIT

Many designers believe the most effective way to use color in a room is by going with a 60–30–10 division. The primary color, usually on the wall or cabinets, should comprise 60 percent of the space. The secondary color, which might include the flooring, should comprise 30 percent of the space, and the accent color, which might be seen on countertops or accessories, should account for 10 percent of the space.

Bold use of color can set the mood, while creating an intense focal point for your kitchen. PHOTO: *Courtesy of CaesarStone* ▼

THE IMPACT OF COLOR

COLOR	FEELING IT INSPIRES	EFFECTS
Yellow	Happy, uplifting, cheerful	Said to help with digestion
Blue	Calming, soothing	Can lower blood pressure, decrease hunger
Green	Tranquil, relaxing	Can lower blood pressure; may reduce allergic reactions to certain foods
Red	Stimulating	Can increase adrenaline, raise heart rate and blood pressure, and induce hunger
Orange	Stimulating, cheerful	Inspires energy, induces hunger
White	Purity, hope	Creates a sense of cleanliness and order
Brown	Warm, casual, comforting	Brings forth a sense of nature, comfort
Black	Elegant, classic	Creates a feeling of depth and richness
Gray	Calming, conservative	Can decrease hunger, but can be depressing if used with a heavy hand

The three colors may be complementary, or contrasting, depending on the goal of the project and the needs of the space. But as a general rule of thumb, you want to go neutral on the bigger expanses and brighter with your accent color.

But what if you love bold colors and don't want to go with a safe look? You might use bright primary colors on painted walls or wall coverings, since these can be easily changed out later.

Countertops, too, are a great place to have fun with color and add visual drama to your kitchen without overwhelming the senses. Or go with a glass tile backsplash in your favorite color to create a striking focal point. And if you're not planning on moving any time soon and have an adventurous streak, why not go for the cobalt blue appliances—or even the fuchsia confetti countertop? After all, it's *your* kitchen. If you're willing to accept the risks in terms of resale value, go for it. Sometimes your style statement has to be about who you are, not what someone else thinks you should have.

Want to know what colors are likely to hold up over the next few years, or even the next decade? The Color Marketing Group (www.colormarketing.org) provides long-term color projections so you can color your world with confidence. ■

THE NEW NEUTRALS

Color *is* one of the fastest ways to make your kitchen look dated. That's why many people who remember their parents' traumatic encounter with a harvest gold refrigerator still lean toward safer, more neutral colors for permanent fixtures.

But today, your choices aren't limited to trendy here-today-hideous-tomorrow hues or boring white and off-white. Neutral colors are becoming more complex, with texture, depth, and dimension that can bring a kitchen to life without being overpowering. Even when bright colors are used, they tend to be softer. For instance, instead of bright red accents, you may see coppery or rustic red stains for cabinetry.

Complex multilayered neutrals are a current twist on classic color themes. Pictured: CaesarStone engineered stone.
PHOTO: *Courtesy of Caesar-Stone*

As a rule, cabinets tend to work best in a neutral shade. But what if you're madly in love with the green- or blue-stained door style you saw on your favorite design show? Try doing a small area such as the base cabinet of the island, or apply green stain to the vintage furniture piece you're refurbishing for your kitchen. Then contrast that with a neutral shade on the rest of the cabinets. Or go with color in the form of stained glass on a few of the cabinet doors. This creates a great visual effect, but is more easily changed out if you hate the color later on. ■

Patterns and Textures

Mix-and-match textures and patterns are central in new millennium style. Many elegant kitchens draw their richness from the balance of textures—the grain of the wood cabinetry, the softly reflective surface of granite countertops, the warm, oil-rubbed bronze finish on faucetry. Don't be afraid to mix anywhere from three to five textures in your kitchen. Natural stone, wood, metal, glass, vinyl, and solid surface or laminate can all add their own unique appeal. But don't go for overkill, either. These textures should contrast but not compete; don't mix several different screaming large particulate patterns in one place. As with color, a little bit of texture goes a long way.

New Millennium Style

Fads are gone in months, the big hot trend in a year or two. But true style has a prevailing direction that can last for decades. The overriding design movement today is away from glitz, high gloss, and gimmicks and toward natural materials that are easy on the eye and psyche. So don't be afraid to bring a little bit of the great outdoors into your kitchen. Whether it's bamboo flooring, natural stone countertops, or lots of green leafy plants to jazz things up, nature never goes out of style.

And speaking of green, it's time to come out of our creative kitchen dreamscape now, and figure out how we're going to pay for all of it.

CHAPTER 5
MONEY ISSUES

Okay, you're ready to make the commitment. No more empty promises, no more banging that turkey on the too-small countertop and announcing to everyone in hearing distance, "I'm *not* going to die in this kitchen!" You've made your decision, and it's time to break open the piggy bank and start shopping.

You open the phone book and look up kitchen dealerships. Conveniently, there's one just a few miles away. And suddenly, there you are, browsing through displays, running your fingers over an exquisite, softly veined granite countertop that feels as cool and smooth as crystal.

Soft music is playing in the background, the smell of freshly baked cookies is wafting through the air, and you know, just *know*, that if you can have this kitchen, these appliances, this fabulous granite countertop, your whole life will be perfect. Your home will be filled

with a smiling *Brady Bunch* family, gathered around the table, eating your perfect made-from-scratch meal while you stack the dishes in your nifty, effort-free dishwasher. And you will be glowing like a new millennium version of Donna Reed (only with better hair and more free time).

In fact, you're already picturing yourself cooking a fabulous Thanksgiving dinner, a *healthy* dinner (thanks to the special steam-infused cooking methods available with the newest, state-of-the art ovens), when you turn around and gasp. It's the price tag, sitting on that kitchen display, ripping apart your fantasy, and slamming you into a state of sticker shock.

Nothing can shatter the dream of the ultimate kitchen like a price tag. There's no two ways about it: New kitchens are expensive. Regardless of what you've seen on *Trading*

When pricing those beautiful cabinets and countertops, remember you're not just pricing the material. You must also take into consideration the cost of fabrication and installation. PHOTO: *Courtesy of Omega Cabinetry* ◀

Spaces, a new kitchen is not something you can pay for with the quarters you keep in your change jar. A new kitchen doesn't have to be out of reach, but like most major expenses, it must be planned for and budgeted carefully.

The Dreaded Budget

After you've wallowed in the fantasy a bit (how else are you going to convince yourself to go for it?), but before you've committed to specific products, you need to do some serious research. This will help you to budget realistically. Don't just look at product prices, though. You also have to look at the details—from those nifty roll-out shelves in the cabinets to the cost of fabricating those stunning ogee-edge countertops.

HOW TO SET A BUDGET AND STICK TO IT

The best way to create a preliminary budget is to start by creating two lists. The first will include all products and services you absolutely *need.* Be honest with yourself: If the refrigerator works just fine, do you really need to upgrade it just because you'd love one of those newer models with flexible storage and a water purifier on the door?

The second list should contain products you'd *like* (sure, you could live with the ugly laminate countertop, since there's nothing actually wrong with it, but you'd really prefer to

As a rule of thumb, a complete kitchen remodel should cost roughly 10 to 20 percent of the fair market value of your home. However, don't be discouraged if you can't invest that much right now. Even with a considerably smaller budget, you can still perform a number of upgrades. ■

upgrade to solid surface). It should also include services you don't absolutely need, but would prefer to contract out (you could probably install your own flooring in a pinch, but you'd rather not).

In Chapter 3, you learned how to measure your kitchen and come up with a layout that will determine how much space you can allot for cabinets, countertops, appliances, etc. Use this list plus your list of needed and desired products, and then do some preliminary shopping.

Web sites can provide you with product features and capabilities, while showroom or home center visits will allow you to see and touch the products and get exact prices. Ask lots of questions. Cabinets, for instance, come in a wide range of prices, depending on what extras you want, and countertops are more expensive if you want the fancy edges.

Once you know what you like, fill out the prices for each product on your need and want

LIST 1
KITCHEN PRODUCTS/SERVICES YOU NEED

PRODUCTS	TYPE	BRAND/MODEL	AMOUNT NEEDED	APPROX. COST
Countertops	_____	_____	_____ linear feet	$ _____
Cabinets	_____	_____	_____ linear feet	$ _____
Flooring	_____	_____	_____ square feet	$ _____
Refrig./Freezer	_____	_____	_____	$ _____
Range	_____	_____	_____	$ _____
Cooktop	_____	_____	_____	$ _____
Wall Oven	_____	_____	_____	$ _____
Microwave	_____	_____	_____	$ _____
Dishwasher	_____	_____	_____	$ _____
Ventilation	_____	_____	_____	$ _____
Wine Cooler	_____	_____	_____	$ _____
Sink	_____	_____	_____	$ _____
Faucet	_____	_____	_____	$ _____
Instant Hot	_____	_____	_____	$ _____
Water Purifier	_____	_____	_____	$ _____
Lighting	_____	_____	_____	$ _____
Hardware	_____	_____	_____	$ _____
Arch. Details	_____	_____	_____	$ _____
PRODUCTS SUBTOTAL				$ _____

PERSONNEL	SERVICES REQUIRED	APPROX. COST
Designer	_____	$ _____
Cabinet Tear Out/Installer	_____	$ _____
Countertop Fabricator	_____	$ _____
Flooring Installer	_____	$ _____
Plumber	_____	$ _____
Electrician	_____	$ _____
Dumpster/Removal	_____	$ _____
SERVICES SUBTOTAL		$ _____
PRODUCTS + SERVICES TOTAL		$ _____
PLUS 15–20 PERCENT MISCELLANEOUS COSTS		+ _____
APPROXIMATE TOTAL BUDGET (LOW END)		$ _____

You may really want a luxury item such as Fisher & Paykel's innovative dishwasher drawers, but make sure you have room in your budget. **DESIGNER:** Gary White, CMKBD, CID (Kitchen and Bath Design) **PHOTO:** Larry Falke ▶

LIST 2
KITCHEN PRODUCTS/SERVICES YOU *WANT*

PRODUCTS	TYPE	BRAND/ MODEL	AMOUNT NEEDED	APPROX. COST
Countertops	_____	_____	_____ linear feet	$ _____
Cabinets	_____	_____	_____ linear feet	$ _____
Flooring	_____	_____	_____ square feet	$ _____
Refrig./Freezer	_____	_____	_____	$ _____
Range	_____	_____	_____	$ _____
Cooktop	_____	_____	_____	$ _____
Wall Oven	_____	_____	_____	$ _____
Microwave	_____	_____	_____	$ _____
Dishwasher	_____	_____	_____	$ _____
Ventilation	_____	_____	_____	$ _____
Wine Cooler	_____	_____	_____	$ _____
Sink	_____	_____	_____	$ _____
Faucet	_____	_____	_____	$ _____
Instant Hot	_____	_____	_____	$ _____
Water Purifier	_____	_____	_____	$ _____
Lighting	_____	_____	_____	$ _____
Hardware	_____	_____	_____	$ _____
Arch. Details	_____	_____	_____	$ _____
PRODUCTS SUBTOTAL				$ _____

PERSONNEL	SERVICES REQUIRED	APPROX. COST
Designer	_____	$ _____
Cabinet Tear Out/Installer	_____	$ _____
Countertop Fabricator	_____	$ _____
Flooring Installer	_____	$ _____
Plumber	_____	$ _____
Electrician	_____	$ _____
Dumpster/Removal	_____	$ _____
SERVICES SUBTOTAL		$ _____
PRODUCTS + SERVICES TOTAL		$ _____
PLUS 15–20 PERCENT MISCELLANEOUS COSTS		+ _____
PLUS TOTAL BUDGET FROM LIST 1		+ _____
APPROXIMATE TOTAL BUDGET (HIGH END)		$ _____

lists. Likewise, get estimates for all services on both lists, and fill them in. Total each list, and add 15 to 20 percent to each for miscellaneous items. The total of the first list (plus the 15 to 20 percent you added) is the low end of your budget. The total of your first list added to the total of your second list would be the high end of your preliminary budget.

Assume your total costs will be at least 15 to 20 percent more than your original budget projections. This way, you're prepared for those extra expenses that creep up. ■

You can also bring your products and services lists to a one-stop-shopping kitchen dealership and ask for an estimate for a complete kitchen. This will give you a good ballpark figure to start with.

Shopping around is a must—and you need to talk to live humans, not just look at price tags. The posted prices can be deceiving if you don't know all the associated costs. Even if you are getting a price for a complete kitchen, be sure to ask what that does (and does not) include. Some may not include such costs as tear out and removal of old cabinets, flooring, or appliances.

If you're refacing cabinets or putting in new countertops, get someone to come into your home, measure, and give you an actual estimate. The difference between what you think is sixteen linear feet of cabinetry but is actually twenty-two linear feet of cabinetry can be quite significant when it comes to dollars and cents. Remember, the more accurate your estimates, the less adjusting you'll have to do to your budget later.

And never forget rule number one: It always costs more than you think it will. So, ditch the rose colored glasses and have a contingency plan (selling kids, spouses, or unwanted relatives on eBay is *not* a good backup budget plan).

The real trick to budgeting effectively is to establish your priorities, and decide up front what you absolutely must have, and what you can live without. Once you know what's on your "gotta have it" list, you can figure out where the best places to cut corners are.

Financing Options

So you've just worked out the budget for your new kitchen, and it's going to cost $24,185—give or take a few thousand dollars. You double- and triple-check your math, but the numbers don't change, and all you can think is, *Oh my gosh, that's a lot of money!*

Okay, breathe. There's no need to hyperventilate. You don't have to sacrifice the kids' college funds, nor will you have to spend the rest of your life with the little dishwasher that could (except when company is over and then it floods the kitchen).

Even if you don't have a kazillion dollars in the bank, you can still remodel your kitchen, thanks to a host of new financing options that make it easier than ever to live well today, and pay for it on the installment plan.

THE OLD OPTION: SAVINGS ACCOUNTS

A mere ten years ago, the majority of people buying a new kitchen saved for it for years, or even decades, and then paid for it out of their hard-earned savings.

Unfortunately, in our credit card generation, many of us struggle with the idea of waiting until we can save what we need in order to have the kitchen of our dreams. Okay, so we don't want to spend our lives perpetually in debt, but if the U.S. government can handle a trillion-dollar shortfall, shouldn't we at least be able to have an oven that doesn't consistently turn out lopsided cakes and half-burnt, half-raw cookies?

But what do you do when you can't live with that peeling linoleum for another day— forget saving for another five years? Or when *you* think you need a new kitchen *now*, but your spouse believes in only spending what you can afford *today?*

Well, good news for you! You don't have to rationalize your lack of patience anymore, because financing not only makes good sense, it makes dollars, too!

New financing options make it easier to get the kitchen of your dreams. This one features a Zodiaq engineered stone countertop. PHOTO: *Courtesy of DuPont Zodiaq* ▲

WHY IT'S SMART TO INVEST IN YOUR HOME

Historically, real estate has always been one of the best investments around. But in recent years, record-low interest rates, rapidly increasing housing values, and a volatile stock market have changed the home improvement landscape to the point where financing your new kitchen isn't just easy, it's also a smart financial move. And the myriad benefits—from financial to professional to emotional—make the whole thing practically guilt free.

Why? Simple. By investing in your home, you increase the value of your house, you increase your future financial stability (because houses are among the smartest investments you can make), and you increase the pleasure you derive from living in your home. Remodeling improves your home's functionality, which is key for those who plan to have children, provide a home for elderly relatives, or "age in place." Investing in your home can also increase your social stature, particularly if you work from home or entertain clients or colleagues there. It's no longer just about impressing the Joneses, it's about making a statement about yourself professionally.

And when was the last time you got to satisfy your inner child, outer professional, *and* accountant—all at the same time?

It's no surprise, then, that financing options have grown by leaps and bounds.

POINT-OF-PURCHASE FINANCING

Home centers and kitchen and bath showrooms frequently offer point-of-purchase financing either through a store or house account. With these, you can make multiple purchases until an established credit line is reached. Or you have the option of an installment loan wherein they work with a lending partner, through which you will take out a loan, and then make principal and interest payments over the term of the loan. A typical loan period ranges from five to twenty-five years.

Store accounts tend to be fastest because you can be approved in minutes. However, be warned, these tend to have higher interest rates, and tax advantages are pretty much non-

Once you decide you're ready for a new kitchen, before you even set foot in a showroom or Home Depot, get your finances in shape. Get a copy of your credit report (you can get this online instantaneously for a nominal fee) and double-check it for problems or mistakes. Repairing credit problems— even if they are mistakes—takes time, so don't leave it until you're ready to start the project. ■

existent. Installment loans may take anywhere from a day to a few weeks to process, but they generally have lower interest rates and the interest may also be tax deductible.

The advantages of point-of-purchase financing include:

■ Convenience—one-stop shopping with no side trips to the bank.

■ Ease of use—someone at the showroom or retail outlet can usually help you through the paperwork.

■ Speed—approvals are usually fast with a minimum of paperwork.

Don't have perfect credit? It may not matter. Remember, kitchen and bath retailers want your business, so it's in their best interest to get you financing. That means they may sometimes be more lenient, or work with borderline credit situations to keep you from taking the job elsewhere.

Have a few skeletons in your financial closet? Don't be embarrassed. Most people don't have perfect credit, and while some blemishes may cost you a few dollars in terms of interest rates, they don't automatically disqualify you from financing. If you have a good relationship with the kitchen dealership, explain that you've had a few blips in the past, and are unsure about your financing. They can run your application through and give you some idea of whether or not the problems are big enough to prevent you from getting the money you need. If you're not comfortable doing this, get a copy of your credit report on your own before doing any serious shopping. ■

As you visit kitchen dealerships and home centers, you will find increasing numbers of retail outlets that offer "no money down" financing.

Be aware that home centers and kitchen dealers often use financing as a way to "upsell" your project. By reducing sticker shock and spreading the payments out over longer periods of time, they may try to upgrade you from lami-

Do all these money issues make you long for a glass of wine? Don't forget to budget for a wine cooler, like this stylish model from Marvel. **PHOTO:** *Courtesy of Marvel* ◄

nate to solid surface, or basic cabinets to semi-custom with all the pull-outs and roll-outs. This isn't necessarily a bad thing. Sometimes it's nice to be able to splurge on a few extras, but be sure you don't spend beyond your means.

HOME EQUITY LOAN

If you've lived in your house long enough to build up equity, a home equity loan is another good option. It's also likely to net better interest rates than many in-store financing programs. In general, you are allowed to borrow up to 80 percent of the equity you have in your

No matter how much it might seem otherwise at the time, "no money up front" is not the same as "free." Don't use financing as an excuse to upgrade the project to something totally beyond your means. ■

home, and the term of these loans generally runs for anywhere from five to twenty years.

The home equity loan involves a fixed rate, which means you know what your payments will be for the entire length of the loan. Many homeowners opt to take out more than they

Pull-outs and roll-outs can be a worthwhile splurge, as they will make your kitchen easier to use for years to come. **PHOTO:** *Courtesy of Rev-A-Shelf* ▶

need and consolidate all their other bills or loans so there's only one monthly payment to deal with. Since home equity loans tend to have significantly lower interest rates than credit cards and other bills, this can actually lower your overall monthly costs, since you're no longer paying steep interest charges and/or penalties.

In order to get a home equity loan, you will have to get an appraisal on your home. This can cost several hundred dollars. However, some banks offer special promotions where they will pick up this cost. The entire loan process can take up to a month.

Some home equity loans might involve a penalty if you prepay them. Different banks have different rates and terms, so it pays to shop around for the best deal. However, if you can lock in a low interest rate, this can be one

Many banks say they offer a home improvement loan, which is actually the same thing as a home equity loan. Don't be confused by the terminology—this is simply marketing. You could, in theory, use the home improvement loan to pay off your car, put money into your business, or buy a whole new wardrobe. They just call it a home improvement loan to encourage you to come in if you're thinking about . . . duh . . . home improvements. ■

of the best options available, and can offer excellent tax advantages, as well.

HOME EQUITY LINE OF CREDIT

The home equity line of credit is similar to the home equity loan in that both require you to go to a bank, fill out an application, and get an appraisal on your home. However, a home equity line of credit is a revolving line of credit. That means, if you get a line of credit for $40,000 to redo your kitchen, and you pay back $20,000 after a year or two, you will still have $20,000 available in credit to use for any other purpose. Once you pay a home equity loan back, you must apply for a new loan if you want to get the money again.

A home equity line of credit comes with a variable rate, which means you generally pay a lower interest rate to start with than you would with a home equity loan. However, that rate can go up over time depending on federal interest rates. A home equity line of credit is best if you're looking to borrow money short term. If you're looking to pay it off over ten or twenty years, you're probably better off with a home equity loan with a fixed interest rate.

REFINANCING YOUR MORTGAGE

Refinancing your home is increasingly popular today as a way to raise cash for everything from paying off credit cards to doing home improvements. If you bought your home before interest

rates dropped, you may be able to get substantial cash up front without significantly increasing your monthly expenses. In fact, you may even be able to *lower* your monthly payments simply because of the difference in interest rates.

Basically, it works like this: If you're looking to take out $50,000, you have your bank redo your mortgage, adding that $50,000 into your existing loan, which then spreads the cost over the term of your mortgage.

The upside: You can have a bunch of cash, right now! Pay off your credit cards, pay off all your bills, get the kitchen of your dreams, and you may even be able to do it without significantly increasing your monthly expenses.

The down side? If you've ever looked closely at your mortgage, you know that no matter how terrific the interest rate, you're still paying a ton of interest. So your $50,000 may cost you $150,000 by the time all is said and done. Refinancing your mortgage also means you end up with less equity in your house. You'll probably have to pay closing costs again. Many banks will allow you to add the closing costs back into your mortgage, but you're still paying them. Since you're effectively applying for a mortgage again, this financing option generally requires more time, hassle, and paperwork than any other one.

SATIN NICKEL VISA

But what if you haven't built enough equity in your home to take out a loan on it, and don't qualify for a consumer financing program? As a last resort, credit cards can help you finance the kitchen of your dreams.

Be very careful, though, because credit card interest rates are traditionally significantly higher than bank loans or home improvement loans, making this an expensive option in the long run. And, if you aren't scrupulous about paying on time, these already-high rates can rocket into the stratosphere. Increasing numbers of credit card companies will now drastically raise your interest rate if you are late on even one payment, and some will even raise your rates if you are late on any payment to any other creditor.

Whatever financing option you choose, check the terms carefully, including any clauses that may cause interest rates to go up suddenly. And, as always, don't sign anything on the dotted line without reading the fine print. ■

You may, however, be able to make this option work if you are only doing it short term.

CASH

But what if you're one of the lucky people who has the money up front? Should you bother with financing?

If you have to use credit cards, you can still keep the costs down if you learn how to successfully navigate The Transfer Game. Apply for a credit card with a low- or no-interest introductory rate (preferably one whose introductory rate remains the same for at least a year) and put the charge on it. Then, right before the introductory rate runs out, get a new card with a similar introductory rate and transfer the balance to that card. Continue this process, changing cards right before the low- or no-interest introductory rate runs out. People have been known to pay little or no interest for years simply by moving balances from credit card to credit card. One caveat: When you move the balance from the old credit card to the new one, be sure to cancel the old card. If you have too many credit cards, it can negatively impact your credit rating. ■

Many financial experts say yes—especially if interest rates are favorable. Financing allows you to retain your cash reserves for emergencies, upgrade a project, and take advantage of tax-deductible interest.

Additionally, if you have to liquidate investments to pay in cash, you will have to pay a capital gains tax on the profit for any liquidated investment. That means it may actually be *more* expensive to pay the project off outright.

But whether you choose to use cash or go with one of the myriad financing options available, the bottom line is that upgrading your kitchen is a smart investment. You'll not only increase the value of your home, but you'll also get to enjoy the benefits of that investment every day, at every meal, for as long as you own your home. And what could be better than that?

Kitchen showrooms are a great place to find new ideas from all over the world, such as this "Fusion" kitchen display, which encompasses a host of international design influences. **DESIGNER:** *Troy Adams (Troy Adams Design)* **PHOTO:** *Courtesy of Troy Adams Design* ◄

CHAPTER 6:
DESIGN ON A SHOESTRING

Cost-Cutting Tips for the Design-Savvy but Financially Impaired

You're standing at the bookstore, thumbing through this thinking, "Well, that's just great, another book for people who are planning to spend $20,000 on their kitchen cabinets! I have $3,000 to spend on my *entire kitchen!* What about me?"

This chapter is just for you. Because good design isn't about how much money you have—it's about how you spend what you have. Remember your starving artist friend's first city apartment? Once you got inside, it was a really great place, right? Bring your friend's inventive spirit to your superecono kitchen remodel.

Maybe you're an urban pioneer who just bought a house in a neighborhood that's undergoing a renewal. The mortgage is eating up all your cash, but you have a lot of style and are willing to dive in, put in some sweat equity, and make a personal statement in a house you're planning to live in for a long time.

Maybe you're a newly married couple who inherited your grandmother's lovely Craftsman home. Unfortunately, a remodeling in the mid-seventies totally messed up the original design elements. You don't have the money to bring the whole kitchen back to its Arts & Crafts glory, but you want to get started.

Maybe you just managed a terrific refinance on the mortgage on your starter home, with a

Okay, it might not look quite this good, but a low-budget design can still have high-end style. **DESIGNER:** *John Sofio (Built, Inc.)* **PHOTO:** *Courtesy of Lone Pine Pictures* ◀

handy cash-out that gives you $10,000 for your kitchen. It's not a lot compared to what some people spend, but it's what you have, and you want to make every penny count. You want to sell this house in a couple of years, and hopefully make a profit.

Here are some hints to make your bargain-basement kitchen just as fabulous as that $260 designer shirt you once found at the outlet mall for $29.95.

Think about how long you're planning to live in your house. If you're in a starter home that you hope to resell in the next few years, don't go crazy with imaginative, individualized designs that potential buyers might not appreciate. However, if this is the find-of-a-lifetime fixer-upper you're going to live in for a long time, go for it. Do something that makes a real design statement, and have some fun. ■

FLOOR MODELS AND OTHER DISCOUNTS

If you know anyone in the design biz, have them keep an eye on any conventions going on in your city. Conventions have displays that cost manufacturers a fortune to ship from their headquarters to the show floor. If you can manage to get on a builders' show convention floor, offer to buy the display of, say, the two lovely high-end cabinets featuring the manufacturer's new wire-mesh glass door for just forty cents on the dollar. They'll probably say yes. And you'll have a great, upscale-looking focal point for your cabinet plan.

This approach can also work locally. If you're shopping in a showroom, take note of the kitchen vignettes on display—especially those that might have been there a while. Kitchen dealers need to update their displays frequently to keep the showroom looking fresh, and when they're ready to change them out, many will sell those displays at a significant discount to make room for new lines.

Collectibles and salvaged items can be great, authentic additions to a vintage or antique look. PHOTO: *Courtesy of Forbo* ▶

SALVAGE

If you're doing a vintage, antique, or other period look, salvaging is a good option.

You can work the salvage market in several ways:

- **Salvage your neighborhood:** Are they tearing down that Craftsman bungalow down the street to put up condos? Is your aunt tossing out her 1940s wood cabinets? Ask if you can have, buy, or barter for those.

- **Salvage through your designer/contractor:** Ask your designer/contractor if they are working on another project which involves tearing out things that would work for you. See if you can purchase these inexpensively.

- **Salvage yards:** In the same way that you can buy used auto parts at a junkyard, there are also architectural salvage yards that offer everything from stone gargoyles to claw-foot tubs to railing spindles, cabinet doors, and more. Just make sure you're knowledgeable about the items you're buying and can correctly gauge their quality—or bring along a vintage-savvy friend.

- **Salvage online:** There are many "old house" Web sites that have message boards with salvageables for sale, or people looking for salvageables to buy. Think of it as an online dating service for your house!

- **Salvage what you have:** Don't forget about recycling your old parts. The cabinets that were too ugly for the kitchen might be just fine for the laundry room or basement storage. That old refrigerator, if still energy efficient, can go in the garage to store all that extra stuff you get at Costco.

- **Salvage it forward:** That appliance you're getting rid of might help prepare some meals at the local Boys/Girls club or soup kitchen. Send your oldies out into the world, where someone else might think they're a great find. You'll make their day, and generate good karma.

FIND OUT WHAT THE PROS KNOW

Products made for professional use are always better than products made for consumers. Get online and start Googling; you'll be amazed at what you can find.

For Urban Industrial or other Contemporary looks, a good source can be a restaurant supply store. These outlets are a wonderland of stuff, both new and used, that's of better quality than most consumer-grade ware, and surprisingly affordable. Makers of store displays, racks, and shelving for manufacturing and industrial use are also a great resource.

DON'T FORGET THE THRIFT STORE

Thrift stores can be another excellent resource, especially if you're going for a Modern Retro look. Older twentieth-century design styles, such as Art Deco, may now be considered antiques, and many 1950s items now have a collectible rather than junk price tag. But the 1960s are still up for grabs. Do your research, and start investigating the thrift stores in your town. Don't look in the cool areas near the college; focus on the older suburban neighborhoods where people are getting rid of stuff in anticipation of retiring. But hurry up, because eventually, word gets out about these things. And when you do find, say, an awesome Danish Modern buffet for twenty-five dollars, try not to jump up and down and act jubilant until you've paid for it and gotten it out of the store!

DIY

Some remodeling projects require more skill than others. It takes an experienced carpenter to build drawers that actually work, for instance. But most people with a reasonable amount of determination, patience, and hand-to-eye coordination can manage to strip and sand, paint and stain, build shelving using pre-cut lumber, and put in their own tile flooring.

The two tools that will make your remodeling life much easier are a cordless drill/screwdriver and an electric orbital sander. If you don't have them, they're a worthy investment. You might also pick up a level, so things don't go sliding off your slightly askew shelves.

The following are two cautionary notes.

First, we do not intend for this chapter to provide *all* the information you need to complete your own DIY kitchen remodel project—that's beyond the scope of this book. We are just giving you ideas and general guidelines. Please get additional information regarding projects such as repainting the kitchen cabinets. There are many, many good books, TV shows, and Web sites available with detailed, step-by-step info about home improvement.

Second, unless you know what you're doing, *do not* try to do your own plumbing and electrical work. Electrocution and flooding are *bad*. Watching Bob Vila on a regular basis *does not* constitute "you know what you're doing." If you have small jobs, you don't need to hire a contractor who's going to charge you thousands of dollars. Instead, find a retired handyman who still does a few little jobs; he'll do just fine with installing your new sink. Or talk to the maintenance guy from your last rented apartment. Many of them are interested in picking up a few dollars on the side working odd jobs.

Make your theme work as camouflage

Use your design style or theme as a starting point for a unique DIY project. Getting creative with inexpensive improvements can make a big difference in camouflaging your kitchen's weak points. For instance, for an Asian look, maybe that big window, which overlooks your neighbor's unsightly garbage cans, could have rice paper applied to it for the look of a backlit shoji screen.

Think outside the box

When looking at options for countertops and storage, don't assume the use of anything has to be what it was originally intended for.

For instance, two refurbished matching dressers or bookcases set back-to-back (with a homemade granite tile top with wood edging) can make an island. Your budget can't swing a fabricated granite top, but you can certainly afford to go down to the tile center and buy twenty twelve-inch tiles, some grout and grout sealer, and attach the whole thing to plywood, right?

Or an armoire or hutch originally intended for clothes can be refinished and used for storing dishes or pots and pans. You can even refinish it to match your cabinetry. The big trend for high-end kitchens is "the furniture look." Well, who says that can't include actual furniture that you found at a yard sale, swap meet, flea market, or street fair?

GET A FOCAL POINT

No one will notice the less fabulous parts of your kitchen if something truly eye-catching is there to draw their attention.

This can be a small item that's far more upscale than what surrounds it, such as an expensive, ultracool faucet to dress up a generic sink and countertop. Or, if you've saved thousands of dollars by painting or refinishing your cabinets, reward yourself. Get some really lovely knobs and drawer pulls that reinforce your theme. You can also add one row of expensive hand-painted tile to your backsplash. Or create a DIY mosaic. Use your imagination.

Alternately, you can spotlight your collectibles to establish a focal point. Country, Shabby Chic, and Retro looks naturally lend themselves to the collectible route, but you can also pull off this look with a contemporary vibe. Let's call it "Urban Ironic." Start with that neon beer sign, campy velvet Elvis painting, or horror movie poster as your centerpiece, and go from there.

People will be so busy staring at all your weird stuff, they won't notice you couldn't afford to replace your refrigerator (which you've camouflaged with a collection of Star Trek-themed magnets, anyway). An unconventional approach to a kitchen also allows you to take hideous things and make them work for you. For instance, if your cabinets are in good shape, but have the most tacky door style you could possibly imagine—wouldn't they look kind of cool if you painted them metallic blue to match that huge stuffed and mounted swordfish you found at the flea market? (Again, this approach is only recommended if you're planning to live

An imaginative tile backsplash can give your kitchen a lot of style. **PHOTO:** *Courtesy of Walker Zanger* ▶

in your house for a long time and don't need to concern yourself with resale value.)

What Are You Going to Do About Your Cabinets?

This is your first big question before you decide what to do. Take a *really good look* at the cabinets you've got. What exactly is wrong with them? Are they structurally unsound, or just ugly? What's ugly about them, the color, finish, door style, or hardware? What are they made of? Are you looking at grimy pressboard that was installed in 1988 or original metal cabinets from the 1950s that could be restored to make a stunning centerpiece for a vintage look?

Vintage metal cabinets can be sandblasted and refinished with automotive-grade acrylic enamel paint, or regular enamel paint with enamel hardener added. ▉

How's the location? Are the cabinets where you want them to be in terms of function? If you're on a micro-budget, you want to keep at least part of your existing cabinets if at all possible. This is especially the case if your cabinets are solid wood. It's a shame to get rid of real wood and put in some MDF (engineered wood) concoction if there's another way.

REFACING

This is the traditional economical approach to remodeling your kitchen on a budget. Having your cabinets refaced will cost approximately half of what replacing them would cost. Refacing also takes less time than a full replacement. If your existing cabinets are solid wood and structurally in good shape, give some thought to going the refacing route. You won't be able to afford anywhere near the same quality in new cabinets, so keep the skeleton intact and just get some new skin.

Typically, the refacers will remove existing cabinet doors, drawer fronts, and hardware. New veneer will be applied to the existing cabinet faces. Many refacers may try to steer you towards laminate, MDF, or other engineered-wood doors. If you want solid wood cabinetry, don't let them put fake doors on your solid wood boxes. Make sure the refacing company even has solid wood (or, at the very least, real wood veneer over good quality plywood) doors, because some don't.

RESOURCES: www.vandykes.com is a restoration site that has a message board where you can trade tips. The same goes for www.oldhouse.com, www.greenspun.com, and www.oldhouseweb.com.

A vintage restoration can be expensive; consider doing your remodel in stages. These nicely understated Merillat oak cabinets are a good place to start.

PHOTO: *Courtesy of Merillat* ▼

Refacing cons

If your kitchen has a poorly designed floor plan, refacing is not going to help you. Your storage and prep space problems will still be there.

There's also a question of warranty about the work done on the existing cabinetry. If something goes wrong in the near future, you can bet the refacing company will figure out

If you intend to do a remodel that keeps with your old house's period style, look into getting a professional restorer for any original solid wood or metal cabinetry. You don't want to do anything to inadvertently damage your soon-to-be vintage treasure. ▪

some way to blame it on your old cabinets, and refuse to fix it for free.

REGLAZING

If your cabinets have a nice door style, but just look kind of old and worn, there are products on the market that will renew a wood finish. These add extra glaze, shine, and depth to the existing stain. You put on one coat and presto, your cabinets look much better. This is an easy and inexpensive option.

OPEN SHELVING

If your cabinets are in good shape, but the doors are ugly, and you can't afford refacing—why not just take the doors off? You'll have clean-lined open shelving that you can refinish any way you want.

This is an option that's only practical if you are a fairly neat, organized person who will stack dishes, cans, and boxes in an eye-pleasing manner—and keep it that way.

If you're doing a real vintage restoration, consider doing your kitchen in parts: maybe replace the cabinets now and the floor and appliances next year. Stick to good-quality products and wait until you can afford the next segment. In the meantime, consider some cosmetic quick fixes like painting an old vinyl floor to spiff up your kitchen. ■

STRIPPING

If your cabinet doors are fine, style-wise, but just have an ugly or worn finish or paint, maybe stripping and refinishing them is the way to go.

WARNING: Stripping is a hard, messy job. Do a patch test first to make sure the wood underneath is worth it. Do not try to strip anything except real wood or vintage metal. Consider the price of hiring a professional for this job versus the time and hassle involved with doing it yourself. We'll say it again. Stripping old paint off a built-in object that you can't turn upside down is hard, messy, arduous work that takes a long time and will probably make you cry at least once. If you are going to embark on this, carefully take off all doors and drawer fronts; it'll make the job somewhat easier. Make sure you have good ventilation, a whole bag of disposable plastic gloves, a twenty-four-pack of paper towels plus rags, and plenty of trash bags.

PAINTING

If your current cabinets have been painted once, you might be able to get away with just doing some basic sanding and priming, and then be able to paint right over them. If there are coats and coats of paint on them, however, you're going to have to strip them even if you ultimately want to repaint them in a solid color.

Do a good job painting your cabinets. Get some old issues of *Family Handyman Magazine*, surf the Net, or ask your brother who practically lives at Home Depot for pointers. Do your research because if you do a quick and sloppy job here, it's not going to turn out the way you'd hoped.

What color should you paint them? That's up to you. For a Shabby Chic, Country, or 1950s Retro look, white-painted cabinets are a classic that will make your kitchen look larger, and give it an airy feel. Remember, painting something a light color will probably take more coats than painting it a dark color.

A subdued color like dark green or taupe that picks up on colors in your countertop or flooring works for a vintage look like Arts & Crafts. For a whimsical theme, a bright color can make your cabinets a focal point; for a dramatic Contemporary or Pacific Rim look, go with glossy black lacquer.

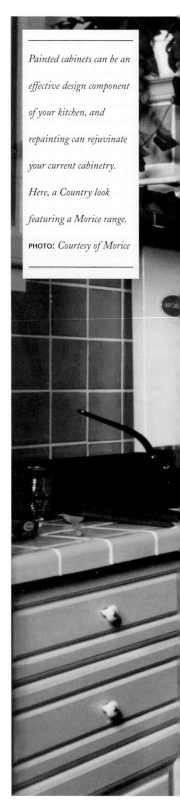

Painted cabinets can be an effective design component of your kitchen, and repainting can rejuvinate your current cabinetry. Here, a Country look featuring a Morice range.
PHOTO: *Courtesy of Morice*

Try a designer finish

Do you yearn for an antique-y look and are skilled at painting? Perhaps you did your bathroom in those textured Ralph Lauren paints and it came out looking great. Or you took a faux finishing class at your home center and successfully applied the technique so it doesn't look like your five-year-old did it. In that case, think about doing your own paint plus a tinted glaze overlay. If you pull it off, it will give your cabinets a look others paid big bucks for.

If you really want to go all out with a Shabby Chic look, try rub through on your cabinets. Paint your existing cabinetry white without previously stripping off any of the existing layers of paint, then use your sander to take off random edges to reveal the old paint for a charming, worn-around-the-edges effect. Some people pay thousands of dollars for cabinets that look like this. With a good dose of sweat equity, you could do it for a couple of hundred.

The Next Phase

Now that you've made a decision about your cabinets, think about the other items in your kitchen.

APPLIANCES

Again, take a good look at what you have. What's wrong with your appliances? Is it func-

When buying basic appliances, remember, the fancy add-on features are probably what are going to break first. For a refrigerator, it's likely to be the in-door ice maker or something similar. A plain, regular, energy-efficient refrigerator from a well-known manufacturer is usually a better choice. ■

tion, or are they just ugly? Maybe much of the ugliness will go away with a good solid scrubbing and some appliance paint. It's been improved in recent years, so it is possible to successfully paint your refrigerator now.

Salvaging your existing fridge can make room in your budget for a new addition you desperately need, such as a dishwasher. If you currently don't have a built-in one, and there are plumbing issues with your house, portable dishwashers—the kind where you roll them over to your sink and attach the hose to the faucet—work just fine.

WARNING: Take energy efficiency into consideration when evaluating the old refrigerator. It works, sure, but it's eating up that electricity like Cookie Monster with a bad case of the munchies. Maybe it's more cost-effective to go get a basic new refrigerator with a better energy rating.

STYLE ALERT: When going for a vintage or retro look, consider a refurbished vintage gas range instead of a new one. An old stove—especially the ones with built-in clocks and other quirky design features—can be a beautiful, evocative focal point for an old-fashioned kitchen. Old gas ranges work just as well for cooking as new models. However, a fully restored antique (which would include replating all the chrome, just like a vintage car) will be just about as expensive as a new one. If you're lucky, you may be able to pick up a functioning range in some used appliance store where they still haven't figured out the difference between "old junk" and "vintage." Get it now, and maybe you can get it replated and otherwise fluffed up sometime in the future when you can afford it. Just be sure to have it checked out by a professional, so you don't end up with a room full of gas.

FLOOR IT

Paint is also a possibility for your current floor, perhaps as a stopgap measure if you're doing your remodel in stages. Industrial floor paint has improved in recent years. If your floor is a hideous color, but is structurally sound, do some research on professional contractors' sites. Go to a pro-oriented paint store and ask for advice. Make sure you get top-quality industrial floor paint.

Generally, the least environmentally friendly paint is the most durable. A lot of environmental regulations are designed so professional contractors don't have to worry about getting sick from breathing toxic fumes every day. But you're only going to paint your kitchen floor once, right? Pay close attention to the directions. If it says sand between coats, or apply primer, make sure you do all that stuff. Otherwise, you'll have a peeling, chipping mess in a couple of months. ■

More Flooring Options

If your design style and budget work with vinyl tiles, this is a job you can definitely do yourself. Self-stick vinyl tiles are an easy project. Just follow the package directions.

It's also possible to put in your own laminate flooring, as well as stone or ceramic tile floors, but these are more complex and expensive projects than self-stick tile. So really think about your skill level before trying to do it yourself. You can also peel off whatever horrible flooring is on there now and see what's underneath. If it's wood, that floor could be resurfaced for a beautiful hardwood look.

WARNING: Resurfacing wood floors is a nasty job, so you might consider bringing in a professional who has a full complement of machinery and skill. We know several urban pioneers who tried to do their own wood floors, and eventually gave up and hired someone.

And there you have it. We genuinely believe that good design should be for everybody, not just people who can afford to hire a designer and buy top-of-the-line products throughout. So get out there and prove us right with a microbudget knockout.

CHAPTER 7

OH BOY, IT'S TIME TO BUY STUFF!

We know some of you went to this chapter first. Because, let's face it, buying stuff is fun, and you want to read about the products. That's okay, we wrote this chapter first, too. We know that shopping is the best part of the kitchen remodeling experience, besides showing off your new kitchen once it's done.

So, here it is, all you ever wanted to know about everything and the kitchen sink.

Cabinet Meeting

We're going to start with cabinets, which are likely to be your most expensive purchase and the cornerstone of your new kitchen. These days, cabinets come in such a wide array of wood species, door styles, finishes, and hardware options, at first glance, you may get that I'm-overwhelmed-and-have-to-go-to-bed-now feeling.

In fact, buying cabinets is a lot like buying a car. Just like you wouldn't walk into a car dealership and say "Hey, let's get the silver one, it's pretty!" don't buy cabinets without checking under the hood, so to speak. Don't just pick a pretty door style.

Since kitchen dealers make the bulk of their money on cabinets, in many instances, the person selling you cabinets will try to get you to buy as many add-ons as possible. To avoid leaving the showroom with the cabinet equivalent of a $799-a-month lease on a two-tone mauve Escalade when all you wanted was a used Honda, you need to have a clear idea of what you want, and what you can afford. Ask yourself these questions:

Cabinets are an investment you'll have for decades, so get the best quality you can afford. DESIGNER: *Gail Drury, CKD/CBD (Drury Designs)* PHOTO: *Kristine Wolff, Kristine Wolff Photography*

STOCK, SEMICUSTOM, OR CUSTOM CABINETS?

Stock cabinets are mass-produced in specific sizes and finishes. You can't modify the dimensions in any way. There have been a lot of advances in computerized woodworking tools that allow manufacturers to produce cabinet parts more quickly, which leads to lower cost. If you can make your kitchen work with stock cabinets, you'll save money. Stock cabinetry doesn't necessarily mean "cheap." Stock just means your kitchen will work with the standard sizes that the cabinet line comes in, and you like the finish that's on the display cabinet.

Semicustom refers to a stock line of cabinets where the manufacturer will make some modifications in height, depth, and width. They might also offer you more options for finishes, trim, and molding. Your cabinets are assembled specially for you, with some made-to-order parts.

Custom isn't quite what it sounds like. You'd think "custom" would mean you show someone a drawing of what you'd like, and they build it, right? For the very high end, and in small local cabinetry shops, it actually does mean that. Elsewhere, custom might mean you can make more changes to the cabinet than you could in the semicustom line in terms of finish, interior storage options, and trims. More exotic woods such as mahogany are also generally only available in custom lines.

SOLID WOOD OR ENGINEERED WOOD?

Many cabinets these days aren't solid wood. Instead, they're engineered wood, laminate- or vinyl-covered particleboard, medium-density fiberboard (MDF), plywood, furniture-grade flakeboard, or some combination thereof. The cabinet door is frequently real wood, with a frame of solid wood, engineered wood or plywood. High-end frameless doors are often plywood with wood veneer exterior surfaces.

This is why you need to decide up front how you feel about synthetic wood. Say you have a limited budget, you don't like imitations, and your current cabinets are solid wood. In this case, you might be better off going with cabinet refacing from a company that offers solid wood replacement doors (for more about cabinet refacing, see Chapter 6). You'll end up with a much better quality cabinet in the end.

On the other hand, if you're thinking, "MDF, thermafoil, laminated, whatever, I don't care what it actually is as long as it looks good," you may want to go with completely new cabinets even if you have a low budget. We know urban pioneers on a microbudget who put stylish contemporary IKEA cabinets in their small kitchen for a couple of thousand dollars, and they look just fine. They may not last forever, but by the time they start to go, the homeowners might be ready for higher-end cabinetry anyway. And by installing all new cabinets, you can rearrange the traffic flow of your kitchen and put the cabinets exactly where you want them.

Now, if you have a generous budget and can afford solid wood in whatever species you want (lucky you!), it's on to the next question.

WHAT WOOD SPECIES AND FINISH?

There are many wood species and all of them take stains, dyes, and glazes differently. Certain species also age, fade, and change from expo-sure to chemicals, heat, or other environmental conditions in various ways. No two pieces of wood are identical. So make sure you see a sample of the specific finish you're choosing *on* the wood species you want, and discuss any environmental factors in your home (such as strong sunlight) with your kitchen dealer.

Beyond that, just pick the species you think looks best with your desired design style.

There are also all kinds of gorgeous exotic wood species that come from the Far East and South America. If you can afford these, the

No two wood pieces are alike, so make sure you see your finish on your wood species. Here, aluminum doors mixed with dark wood cabinets for an unusual, eclectic effect.
PHOTO: *Courtesy of Element Cabinets* ◀

WOOD SPECIES AT A GLANCE			
Maple Currently the most popular species for cabinets, light, very even grain	**Cherry** Also currently popular, fine grain, more reddish than maple	**Hickory** Wild, distinctive grain, great for a Rustic or Southwest look	**Mahogany** Very hard, dark reddish wood, exotic, imported, often expensive
Alder Similar to maple but cheaper and more readily available	**Oak** Light, medium grain, a cabinet mainstay; quarter-sawn oak is great for a historically accurate Arts & Crafts look.	**Walnut** Darker, less red tone than mahogany, growing in popularity with current trend toward darker woods	**Lyptus** Similar to mahogany but more affordable

fabulous professional designer you've surely hired will tell you all about them.

And then we get to finishes. Again, it all depends on your budget and preference. For stock or semicustom cabinets, you'll have a wide variety of stains, glazes, and colors to choose from. All stains and finishes are not usually available for all cabinet door styles. So remember, if you start with, "I want *that* stain on *this* door," it will likely cost extra, as will a glaze overlay or other multistep finish treatment.

If you have a limited budget, we recommend you get a basic clear or translucent finish and let the beauty of the wood speak for itself.

STYLE ALERT: Glaze overlays have been the big trendy thing for the past few years. Glazes are transparent or semitransparent stains that are applied after the sealer coat. Glazes can be used to enhance carvings or create other decorative effects, give the cabinet door more dimension, or act as as a top coat over the finish. Like stains, dye, and paint, glazes will look different on different types of wood. Be sure you see the color on your choice of wood before you order.

WHAT DOOR STYLE?

As you can see, there are many available door styles—square doors, arched doors, framed, frameless, recessed, raised, and beadboard. Manufacturers tend to name their doors, so they'll be talking about the "Côte d'Azur" and the "Wellington" while you're trying to figure out how that compares to the "Dover" from the other showroom.

To further confuse you, doors also come in inset, lipped, and full overlay. But, while there are many door styles, there are only three basic types: raised panel, recessed panel, and slab.

The raised panel has a raised section in the

DIAGRAM 4.5 CABINET DOOR STYLES

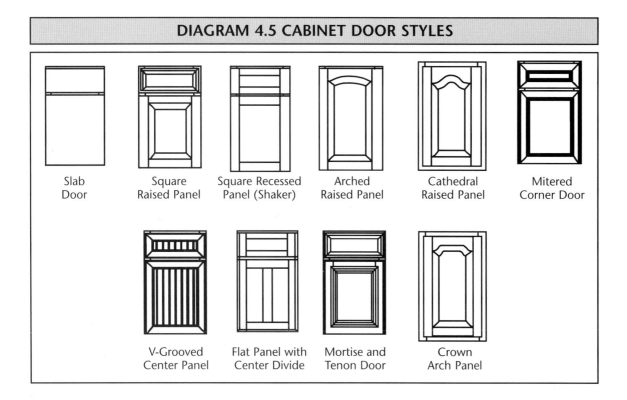

Slab Door
Square Raised Panel
Square Recessed Panel (Shaker)
Arched Raised Panel
Cathedral Raised Panel
Mitered Corner Door

V-Grooved Center Panel
Flat Panel with Center Divide
Mortise and Tenon Door
Crown Arch Panel

middle that can be square, curved, or arched. This door gives a kitchen a more traditional look. Curved raised panels also tend to make your kitchen look busier, because it's less of a clean line.

The recessed panel is frequently a framed door. It has what's called the "face frame" around the cabinet door, which usually is made of the same wood species. Less expensive cabinets will have engineered wood or plywood face frames, while better cabinets will have solid wood frames.

The slab door is just what it sounds like— a plain door and generally frameless. It gives you a smooth line that works with all kinds of Contemporary or Modern Retro looks.

Which door is right for you? If you have a mid- to high-end budget and are hiring a designer for your kitchen, you have the option of almost any door style. We could go on for another twenty pages here about acanthus corbels, moullion doors, carvings, miters, onlays, finial pediments, crown valances, inset light rails, and beaded inserts. All of these are generally custom options that will cost more.

If you have a micro-to-mid budget and are a DIY or buy-it-yourselfer, we recommend something uncluttered and classic like the Shaker—a plain framed recessed panel door— or a frameless slab door. Your kitchen cabinets are going to be with you for a long time, so refrain from the trendy or gimmicky.

Raised panel doors give your cabinetry a traditional look.

DESIGNER: *Mary Jo Peterson, CKD, CBD, CMG (MJ Peterson Designs)* ▲

STYLE ALERT: At the high end, glass doors and metal inserts in framed doors are now considered a hot trend. Glass doors break up the monotony of a long row of cabinet doors, can showcase collectibles, and can also enable you to do interesting design details with lighting behind the door. Glass front doors are available in all kinds of options like frosted, etched, and wire mesh. For metal inserts, perforated stainless is increasingly popular, along with metal designs in copper and bronze shades.

HARDWARE, ACCESSORIES, STORAGE, AND RECYCLING OPTIONS

Knob mania! Kitchen cabinet hardware comes in so many styles and finishes, it's practically impossible to mention them all—big knobs, small knobs, thousands of knobs. Want a pewter knob that looks like a pineapple? An oil-rubbed bronze bar pull? An authentic-looking vintage glass knob? Historically accurate Mission hardware? A contemporary stainless "t" pull? Lalique crystal? If you want it, someone's got it.

RESOURCES: www.kitchencabinethardware.com, www.myknobs.com, www.restorationhardware.com

A place for everything— and we do mean everything!

You know that money you're saving by passing up the distressing, lavender frost glaze, beaded inset, and angel carvings the kitchen dealer was trying to talk you into? Here's your chance to spend it on a worthy add-on. Today's kitchen storage systems are complex, well-made, and stylish. They're a big improvement on the old plastic cutlery tray and creaky lazy Susan of yesteryear.

Remember when you bought that huge organizer thingie for your office, and all of a sudden you could find your Post-it pads and your scissors? The same thing can happen to your kitchen.

The following is a list of overall storage trends.

■ **Fewer built-in cabinets, more furniture pieces.** Furniture pieces are actually more economical than built-in cabinets these

Glass doors are available in all kinds of options, such as this striking green tint. PHOTO: *Courtesy of Architectural Glass Effects* ▲

days, plus, if you're putting in pricey storage features, you can take them with you when you move.

■ **Fewer base cabinets, more deep base drawers.** Much more convenient than getting down on your hands and knees and digging around for that weird pan you use once a year. Large dowels help organize pots and pans, lids, and dishes.

■ **Self-closing mechanisms, heavy-duty slides.** Because drawers now weigh about a thousand pounds.

■ **Pull-outs and pull-downs.** These features bring pots and pans out of that back cabinet, or down from way up high, with the

Can you ever have too much storage? **DESIGNER:** *Steven Naphtali (Kitchen Expressions of Short Hills)* **PHOTO:** *Daniel Aubry, New York City* ▶

push of a button. They are especially helpful if someone in your family has a disability.

- **Wastebasket pull-outs.** Make sure you get large enough containers. In many areas, recycling is mandatory, and you have to separate paper products, glass, plastic, and regular trash. If you have a busy family, go with one big base pull-out per recyclable category. Arrange them to either side of your sink. For smaller amounts of trash, the two-bins-in-one-pull-out will work for you. Avoid the small four-bins-per-pull-out unless you're a single condo dweller, or you'll be taking out the trash every hour on the hour.

- **Pull-outs for small spaces.** European manufacturers have some amazing space savers, such as six-inch-wide, but very tall, pull-outs. Sometimes, it's hard to find this stuff in the United States but it's worth it if you have a cramped condo space.

- **Better quality and style.** No more plastic, except for clear Plexiglas (great for storing spices and other items where you need to read the label). Today's quality storage systems are made of wood, chrome, stainless steel, or brushed aluminum, and adjustable so you can customize your space.

■ **More top cabinet undermounts.** Microwaves, TVs, and other small appliances can now move off the countertop, giving you more work space. If you really want to get fancy, consider the iCEBOX information/communication/entertainment appliance. This innovative space saver includes TV, Internet access, DVD player, radio, and hook-up to surveillance system.

Counter Fit

There is a huge array of countertop materials to choose from these days, and all have different uses and benefits.

Here are some points to remember when choosing a countertop:

■ **Functionality and price.** Revisit the messiness quiz in Chapter 2 and think about your functionality requirements as well as your budget. Your countertop can cost anywhere from a couple of hundred bucks to thousands.

■ **Mix and match.** A look that encompasses two or more different countertop materials is extremely chic right now. You can also achieve a more expensive look than your budget suggests. Pick the segment of your countertop that's going to be the focal point and splurge on your high-priced material here. Or use the more expensive material as an accent, such as a border of hand-painted or metal tile on a basic tile countertop.

■ **Get the edge.** Your countertop will be custom-fabricated, so you can get anything—from an ornate edge like the double ogee to no edge treatment at all—for the rugged look of rough-cut stone. Remember, the more complicated and time-consuming the edge treatment, the more pricey. If you

COUNTERTOP MATERIALS AT A GLANCE

MATERIAL	PROS	CONS
Granite: The new countertop classic for the high-end kitchen, is compatible with many design styles.	Gorgeous, luxurious, elegant. Since it's a natural material, no two slabs of granite are 100 percent alike. Many prefer to pick out their own slab. It's also very durable, burn-proof, nonporous, and stain-resist-ant—*if it's sealed properly,* generally about once a year.	It's pricey; *so* popular in recent years, it doesn't have the elite appeal it once did. Highly polished granite may be too glitzy for some design styles. Honed granite is less shiny, but higher mainte-nance. Fabrication takes longer than solid surface.

COUNTERTOP MATERIALS AT A GLANCE

MATERIAL	PROS	CONS
Engineered stone: We give engineered stone a gold star as one of the best new products of recent years. Thoroughly disproves the old adage that fake equals cheap-looking and tacky.	Primarily made from quartz, looks 99.99 percent exactly like granite. It even has the cold touch of stone. Available in colors that Mother Nature didn't include in her granite catalog, such as blue. It has a consistent pattern, so has fewer fabrication issues than natural stone. Hard, durable, low maintenance, and almost spill-proof, it doesn't have to be resealed, ever—now available in honed finishes.	Because it is so much like real stone, engineered stone costs almost as much as real stone does, and has to be fabricated in the same way.
Solid surface: This is the indestructible workhorse of the countertop family—low maintenance and high durability.	Nonporous, stain and heat resistant, it prevents growth of bacteria in food prep areas. Lends itself to easy-to-clean integral sinks and original edge treatments. Solid all the way through; renewable, and comes in many inventive patterns and textures—including matte surfaces.	Cheaper than granite or engineered stone, but not by much. Unlike engineered stone, "granite look" solid surface will never be mistaken for the real thing, especially after you touch it (so choose a "synthetic and proud" original pattern).
Ceramic tile: The original countertop material, and still one of the best. A classic that fits beautifully with everything from rustic Mediterranean to Transitional to stark Contemporary minimalist.	Virtually limitless design possibilities: any size, shape, color, or design from tiny mosaics to big squares, triangular, octagonal, hexagonal, or any bizarre custom tile you can imagine. Economical, your best bet for an authentic antique look on a limited budget—high heat resistance, too.	Grout provides a crevice for dirt and also tends to stain. Grout sealers have improved in recent years; make sure you get a top quality one. Still, stain- and scratch-resistance not as good as some other materials mentioned.
Laminate: An economical and popular choice for countertops, available in many beautiful, confidently man-made designs.	Available in just about every pattern and color imaginable, including the humorous or downright bizarre, as well as personalized custom patterns. If you have a whimsical design style, here's your chance to go crazy with your kitchen.	Low maintenance, but not as durable as some other materials. May eventually get burns, scratches, and chips, and, unlike solid surface, cannot be resurfaced. *Avoid fake-looking reproductions of natural materials.*

COUNTERTOP MATERIALS AT A GLANCE

MATERIAL	PROS	CONS
Concrete: A trendy, high-end, very customized choice	Each piece is custom made, and you can have anything you want. A concrete fabricator can make your slab look like the wizened, crumbling terra cotta of a Tuscan farmhouse, a sandy beach complete with embedded shells, or the glossy, minimalist galley of a space station.	Has maintenance issues. Concrete sealed with penetrating sealer still has to be buffed and waxed monthly, and stains wiped up quickly. Epoxy coating makes it impenetrable but changes the look. (Think bar-top coating versus butcher block.)
Stainless steel: Great for a no-nonsense professional-style kitchen look	Gives a cool industrial vibe that says you're really, really serious about cooking.	Too much steel gives your kitchen an armor-plated, cold feel. Also tends to scratch, so get a brushed or textured finish for a hard-working countertop.
Butcher block/sealed wood: A great complement to serene, natural Zen, Country, or Rustic looks	Natural oil-treated butcher block is gorgeous, but must be cleaned properly to avoid bacteria from setting in.	Has maintenance issues. As with concrete, wood can be sealed to make it impenetrable, but that thick shiny coating makes the look more bar top than country house.
Granite tile: If you love real granite but can't afford it, granite tile will get you that look.	Available for as little as $10 per 12"x12" tile.	Requires grout, complete with its staining and dirt-attracting properties. Top-quality grout sealer is a must
Marble: An elegant, classic material	A beautiful, luxurious look	Is very susceptible to scratching and staining—more appropriate for bathroom or backsplash.
Limestone and slate: Matte, elegant, subtle stone surface	Lovely in a more rugged, back-to-nature, Zen way; unusual and trendy	Has maintenance issues similar to marble and concrete—not for messy people.

have small children or older relatives, a rounded edge is probably more suitable.

■ **Be synthetic and proud.** When choosing solid surface or laminate, avoid the boring, tacky pseudogranite and go for a color or pattern *not* found in nature. Pair it with a

Contemporary or "Post-*Jetsons*" Modern Retro look, and you'll have a cool, highly functional, and durable countertop.

WARNING: Concrete countertops are beautiful and a hot trend. Unfortunately, since the setup costs for a precast concrete shop are

CaesarStone engineered stone is now available in a less shiny, honed finish—a boon for those who love the look of a concrete countertop, but want lower maintenance.

PHOTO: *Courtesy of Caesar-Stone* ▶

COUNTERTOP EDGES

Setback

Spanish

Eased

Classic

No Buildup

Double Classic

Double Eased

1/2 Bullnose

Bevel

Full Bullnose

Double Bevel

Triple Head

Coved

Even Receding

Full Bullnose Inlaid

Inlaid with Corian or Other Material

1/2 Bullnose Inlaid

Recessed inlaid with Tile

Double Bevel Inlaid

Ogee

countertop resources: www.chengdesign.com, www.kingsgrant.com, www.formworks-nc.com, www.soupcan.com, www.buddyrhodes.com

Concrete allows creative flexibility other materials don't, for example, this innovative countertop by Fu-Tung Cheng. DESIGNER: *Fu-Tung Cheng (Cheng Design)* ▲

Major and Minor Appliances

Okay, ready for your next big purchase? Like cabinets, appliances are the big-ticket item in your remodel.

much lower than stone fabrication, the business is attracting inexperienced, fly-by-night people. Make sure you get a fabricator who knows what he or she is doing. Many good fabricators belong to the National Precast Concrete Association (www.precast.org). Other concrete

◼ Prioritize your appliances. Which ones get everyday use that justifies the extra bucks to get the top-of-the-line product? If most of your family's meals come hot off the George Foreman grill, you don't really need a beau-

Solid surface comes in many inventive colors and textures such as this stylish blue countertop from Staron. PHOTO: *Courtesy of Staron* ▲

tiful $3,000 professional-style oven just to make Thanksgiving turkey once a year.

■ Spend on your priorities. If fresh, healthy food is important to you, that built-in veggie steamer for your cooktop is a fine choice, even if that means you have to pass the satin nickel wall-mounted electric plastic wrap dispenser. For your heavily used

appliances, you want plenty of power, and extra features to make your life easier. Look for a reliable machine that's well made and as top-of-the-line as your budget allows.

■ Know the truth and avoid expensive mistakes. When researching appliances, look at consumer-run complaint Web sites, don't just take your kitchen dealer's recommendation.

Some luxury appliances may be temperamental, while other less glamorous but economical brands may turn out to be supremely reliable and hard-working.

HOME ON THE RANGE

You have far more choices than your parents' and grandparents' generations when it comes to cooking appliances. They just bought a stove, and there it was. Now, you can have a range and/or a cooktop and/or a wall oven and/or a convection oven. Again, think about your functionality requirements.

- **Going Pro.** If you're an enthusiastic cook or if you entertain frequently, you probably desperately want a pro-style range, and with good reason. The higher temperatures and other features of a professional range allow you to do things ordinary stoves can't, and really can take you to the next level—from dabbler to serious chef.

- **Gourmet or convenience features?** Professional ranges have many advantages, but generally do not include consumer-friendly "push this button and the appliance will work like magic" features. That's because gourmet cooks tend to prefer a hands-on, primal cooking experience.

- **Are you a control freak?** Some people like appliances that can be programmed to do

Appliances will make up a significant portion of your kitchen budget. Here, a high-end Sub-Zero drawer system. PHOTO: *Courtesy of Sub-Zero* ◄

A pro-style range such as Thermador's, featuring a built-in griddle, can do things consumer-grade appliances cannot. PHOTO: *Courtesy of Thermador* ►

all sorts of zippy things in timed sequence, and then shut themselves off. If you prefer appliances that go ON/OFF, Low-Medium-High, avoid models whose controls look like the deck of the starship *Enterprise*.

- **Your oven can be anywhere.** The oven used to be joined to the cooktop, but no longer. You can have your cooktop on your island, and your oven on the wall. If you don't use your oven that much, tuck it someplace outside of the primary work area.

TOYS IN THE HOOD

If you're getting a pro-level range, you need a pro-level vent hood. If you don't, your kitchen

will continuously be setting off the smoke alarm because a regular vent just won't be able to handle the BTUs you're cranking out. Here's what to remember about today's new and improved vents:

■ **Use the vent as a stylish focal point.** Vents used to always be big, boxy steel things—

only a design plus if you were going for an Urban Industrial look. But now, you can get a powerful vent in many stylish varieties and materials such as glass or copper. In fact, more and more people are putting their cooktops on their island, and making the vent hood their kitchen's centerpiece. If

Vent hoods do not have to be huge—Gaggenau's pop-up op-vent arm does the job just as well. **PHOTO:** *Courtesy of Gaggenau* ▶

you don't want your vent to be the focal point, consider a front around it in, for instance, wood or stucco.

■ **Keep cleaning in mind.** Your vent will get filthy from a combination of oil/food particles/soot. So remember, ornate appliqués are much harder to clean than curved glass or metal. Consider a dishwasher-safe filter for easier cleaning.

■ **Listen to your vent.** Consider the noise factor. Generally, the bigger and stronger the vent action, the louder it is. Make sure you turn on your vent before you buy it, and avoid those whose roar reminds you of the "Nuclear Testing Wakes Up Huge Monster and Boy Is It Mad" movies from the 1950s.

■ **Remember the lighting.** The hood will be illuminating your cooktop, and halogen lights are a nice option here.

COLD STORAGE

How much refrigerator space do you actually need? Don't automatically opt for the SUV-sized model. If you use a lot of fresh food, you can't buy it that far ahead of time, right?

■ **Consider a separate extra big freezer instead.** If you're a heat-and-serve kind of family, more freezer space will allow you to

stock up on those just-add-meat stir-fry meals.

■ **Measure inside and out.** Refrigerator energy guidelines changed in 2002, and a number of manufacturers dropped older models from their lines. Since new models are required to have more insulation, there's less interior space.

■ **Going the modular route?** If you're opting for multiple undercounter refrigerators, make sure they all have enough venting if you're putting them in locations that do not have an open air flow—or the refrigeration systems won't work properly.

■ **Go retro, sort of.** If you're doing Modern Retro or another period design style, check out appliance reproductions that have a vintage look, but all the modern features inside.

■ **Coolio.** White wine drinkers, rejoice. Temperature-cooled wine is now an affordable (under $500) mass-market item—a great component to your beverage station module. Combine it with a room-temperature rack for reds. More upscale models with added features are available, as well.

■ **And for beer drinkers,** consider an undercounter-size refrigerator beer station.

Elmira's 1950s reproduction fridge is a great pick for a Modern Retro look. A matching stove is also available.

PHOTO: *Courtesy of Elmira* ▶

You buy beer by the keg, stick the keg in the fridge part, and beer comes out the tap on top.

THE FINISH LINE

Unless you've recently been released from an Envirodome experiment, you know that stainless steel has been all the rage for appliances for the last few years. But real steel is a fingerprint magnet, too. New stainless-steel look finishes, like Whirlpool's Satina, give you the look without the maintenance. Also consider the total square footage in your kitchen that will be steel. Avoid that medical examiner's autopsy room vibe!

- **Metallica.** The very high-end appliance market offers warm-toned metal finishes like copper, as well as aluminum, which gives you a light, airy feel.

- **Go classic with black or white.** Good old white still has a nice, classic feel; black perennially looks sleek and sophisticated, especially when paired with blond wood cabinetry.

- **Consider integral fronts.** A panel that matches your cabinetry to cover the front of your refrigerator, dishwasher, or wine cooler is a great option if you're going for a streamlined, uncluttered look, or a very woodsy, natural, or antique style. Just remember, the more custom appliqués and

Steel is the new neutral for appliances. **DESIGNER:** *Bruce Zickuhr, AIA (Metropolitan Designs)* **PHOTO:** *Richard Sprengler* ▲

finishes you add to a cabinet door, the more expensive it is. And all that expense transfers over to your integral fronts, too.

YOUR FRIEND, THE DISHWASHER

Okay, now we're going to get to the Kill 'Em All Dishwasher—the powerful, able-to-eviscer-ate-burned-on-spaghetti-sauce-at-a-hundred-paces monster that will keep your kitchen from getting away from you. Because you know that nothing is more disheartening than walking into a kitchen with dirty dishes all over the place. You also need a dishwasher that will take all kinds of rinsing techniques and still remain victorious. You want your kids to help load the

The Kill 'Em All Dishwasher

will be your best friend.

PHOTO: *Courtesy of Viking* ▶

dishes without having to do it over later, right? So leave plenty of room in your budget for an excellent dishwasher.

- **In fact, consider getting *two*.** Dishwashers today are actually cheaper than cabinets, so consider dishwashers as perpetual moving storage. You get clean dishes out of one, put dirty dishes into the other. When the second one is full, you wash those dishes. Then you unload any remaining dishes out of the first one, and put them in the cabinet. Notice, you didn't have to put most of them on the shelf, saving yourself a step.

- **Think mini.** If you live in a cramped condo, or you just don't eat at home much, consider something like the Briva In-Sink Dishwasher or Fisher & Paykel's dishwasher drawers.

SMALL APPLIANCES

When choosing small appliances, again, think of what kind of food you really cook. It's nice to have a bread maker, but if your idea of gourmet cooking is adding extra shrimp to Trader Joe's shrimp pasta primavera in a heat-and-serve bag, are you *ever* going to bake your own bread? Consider your counter space and budget. Then pick one or two small appliances that you will actually use and make sure you get good, reliable brand-names.

- **Speeding to dinner.** Gourmet isn't your priority; serving meals that didn't come from the drive-through is. You might love a speed-cooking oven. "Speedies" mix microwave and conventional cooking technology, giving you food cooked at microwave speed, but without the wilted microwave taste of old. We give speedies a gold star, especially since they have gone down in price considerably in the last few years.

- **More speedy options:** Whirlpool's Polara is a free-standing range that also has a refrigeration function, and can be programmed to keep a raw, ready-to-cook meal refrigerated until a preprogrammed time. Once it's cooked, it will keep the food warm for an hour, then refrigerate it again. And GE's Artica refrigerator has both an express chill and express thaw feature.

- **Don't skimp on your microwave.** You probably use the microwave every day, so a top-of-the-line model—or even two—is a worthy investment. Microwaves come in 1100- and 1200-watt models for more power, and are now available in stainless steel, along with nice, designer matte finishes that will coordinate with your design theme.

The Great Outdoors

Looking for a truly different, new kitchen innovation? Your choices are as wide as the great outdoors. In fact, the latest, greatest thing under the sun . . . is actually under the sun, as today's kitchens move outside with increasingly sophisticated setups that may include multifunction, high-powered grills with warming drawers, refrigerators and wine units, weather-proof cabinets, countertops, sinks, and dishwashers.

Live in Wisconsin? No problem! Outdoor kitchens aren't just for people in tropical climates. Elaborate patio heaters, rolling carts, weather-proof materials, and other innovations have made the outdoor kitchen a viable alternative for even cold-weather folks. After all, if you can enjoy the taste of summer year-round, why not?

So, what's so great about having an outdoor kitchen? Here are three great reasons to take the party outside:

1. **Food tastes better outdoors.** Is there anything better than eating a perfectly cooked, hot-off-the-grill steak while watching a fabulous sunset with friends?

2. **Guys love it.** Even the most cooking-averse male tends to come to life when given the chance to grill up some burgers or steaks. In fact, outdoor kitchens are a

natural evolution in the trend toward men becoming more active in the cooking process.

3. **You can be a show-off.** What fun is a fabulous kitchen if only people you know and like get to see it and envy your great taste? Here's a chance to flaunt it to the whole neighborhood.

■ **Start with the grill,** either freestanding or built-in. Movable units are best for colder

The outdoor kitchen is today's newest status symbol. **PHOTO:** *Courtesy of Viking* ▼

A grill, such as this luxury model from Viking, is the functional centerpiece of your outdoor kitchen. **PHOTO:** *Courtesy of Viking* ▲

weather climates, while built-in grills work best in warm-weather climates, or in areas that are fully covered. Of course, everyone knows when it comes to barbecuing, it's all about the fire. The newest outdoor grills are hot, hot, hot, with more BTUs than ever before. Serious chefs will also welcome the wide array of add-on options, from woks to warming drawers, side burners, smokers, and griddles. Many outdoor grills can be purchased with a cart that not only functions as an island but also includes side shelves and storage drawers to keep things tidy.

■ **Built-in refrigeration** is also a great way to keep the party going strong. Built-in beverage or wine refrigerators offer convenient access to cold beverages and keep wines at optimum temperatures. You can also use an outdoor refrigerator to keep meats cool until it's time to put them on the grill or store condiments without worrying about them spoiling in the heat. Beer tappers, too, are perfect for the party-hearty type. Several manufacturers of built-in refrigeration offer a variety of models, perfect for gatherings of all sizes.

- **A sink and a dishwasher** will make cleanup a snap, even if you want to do a fancy gathering with china and real silverware instead of the traditional outdoor barbecue paper plates and plastic utensils.

- **Weather-proof cabinets** allow you to store everything from cooking utensils to hamburger buns. Several companies also offer a line of modular components—similar to those of an interior kitchen—with everything from cabinets and refrigeration to sinks and lighting. These complete units take the work out of creating your dream outdoor kitchen. Outdoor cabinets are frequently made of plastic/wood composite (like Trex for your deck), steel, or a hard wood like mahogany, redwood, or teak.

- **A note about materials.** While outdoor kitchens allow for greater style flexibility,

you should still look for durable materials such as stainless steel, tile, stucco, brick, stone, and concrete.

- **The price tag.** Complete outdoor kitchens can run from a couple of thousand dollars to $60,000 and up, depending on how elaborate you want to go. While it's fun to splurge on some of the luxury extras, if money is tight, invest the bulk of your budget in a high-quality, high-power grill.

That Sinking Feeling

The sink, that's a pretty simple category, right? Not any more. Your sink can be basic, but it can also practically become a full-fledged appliance with grates, basket strainers, colanders, and drain boards to make it more efficient and high tech. The choice of materials, styles, and finishes has also expanded.

- **Think function.** Your kitchen sink is arguably the hardest-working spot in your house. Nothing else gets as much use and abuse. But you still want a style that goes with the overall look of your kitchen.

- **Think big** if you have a good-sized kitchen. Ten inches is the current favored depth rather than the previous standard seven inches—to better fit that giant pasta pot,

Today's sinks have many options such as colanders and drain boards. Here, a striking two-bowl Blanco model.

PHOTO: *Courtesy of Blanco* ▶

SINKS AT A GLANCE		
MATERIAL/STYLE	**PROS**	**CONS**
Stainless steel: Today's overwhelming choice, comprising 75 percent of the kitchen sink market	Extremely durable, especially a brushed or textured finish that doesn't show scratches. Perfect for many design styles and grid add ons.	Not compatible with many antique, rustic, or country looks. Polished steel is susceptible to scratches and fingerprints.
White: The best choice for accurate antique and vintage looks	A durable, beautiful classic in fire clay or vitreous china	Avoid cast iron, which is much less durable today than in older lead-filled models.
Integral solid surface or concrete	Makes for very easy cleaning, gives a clean uncluttered line	A more complex fabrication, especially for concrete
Undermount sink	The perfect style for contemporary looks, shows off countertop material, easy to clean	A distinctly contemporary look that doesn't work with antique design styles
Drop-in sink	A classic look, often more economical than other styles	Crevice around edge tends to catch dirt
Farmer sink	The perfect centerpiece for a country or rustic look. Best in white china or fire clay.	Takes up more space than undermounts or drop-ins, looks busy
Granite composite and engineered stone	The look of stone for a sink, two new material choices	As with steel, you can have too much of a good thing. Make sure you don't have so much stone in your kitchen it looks like the Flintstones'.

turkey roaster, and other megacookware. Remember that a lot of your better cookware has to be hand washed because the dishwasher is too harsh on the nonstick coating.

- **Don't fear color.** If you really want a sink in a color other than white, steel, or bisque, go for it and don't worry about resale value. Sinks are fairly easy to change out, and relatively inexpensive. No one will pass on buying your house because they don't like the kitchen sink color.

- **Think accessories.** What sink accessories do you really need? Again, it depends on your budget and the way you cook. If money is no object, you might as well get everything from the antique pewter soap dispenser to the snap-in cutting board. But even on a limited budget, the bottom grid is a good idea, because it will protect your sink. Plus, think of an additional accessory that would make you happy, such as a hot water dispenser for cold-weather climates.

The Faucet

The faucet is a focal point, similar to a stunning piece of jewelry that can make a budget cocktail dress look like it came from a designer's couture collection. Like your door hardware, the faucet is a way of getting a lot of

design bang for your buck—so get something special that you really love.

Some points to remember about faucets:

- **To pull or not to pull?** Do you want a pull-out spray to come out of your central faucet, or from the side, or are you not particularly concerned about the pull-out? Pull-outs have improved in recent years, with sturdier hoses, many of which are now practically indestructible. A pull-out is great for hand-washing dishes, plus it opens up a spot in your sink's four-hole configuration for something else, such as the hot water or filtered water dispenser. Remember, pull-out faucets look terrific in contemporary kitchens, but anachronistic and inappropriate in all others.

- **Consider the high arc.** If you do a lot of cooking with big pots, consider a high-arc faucet. It's also more showy, which works with our strategy of getting a great faucet that makes your sink and countertop look more expensive.

■ **So many finishes, so little time.** For years, faucets used to be polished chrome, just like ice cream was vanilla. And now, there's Ben and Jerry's, and there's a cornucopia of finishes for your kitchen faucet.

Water, Water, Everywhere

If you live in a major metropolitan area, you know your water quality is scary. You don't know where it's been, what's been in it, or what chemicals were used to remove what's been in it. Undoubtedly you already have some way of getting drinkable water. Maybe it's the pitcher in the fridge, cases of water from Costco, or an office-style water cooler.

But maybe you still worry about cooking with unfiltered water, or giving it to your 120-pound Akita (a very sloppy drinker who goes through gallons of the stuff). A built-in water filtration system may be just the thing. Some questions to ponder:

FAUCET FINISHES AT A GLANCE		
MATERIAL	PROS	CONS
Chrome: A classic that's making a comeback	Very durable, inexpensive, perfect for retro and vintage looks as well as Urban Industrial	Polished chrome shows fingerprints and smudges; too shiny for many serene, natural design styles
Brushed and satin nickel: The star-is-born finish of the past two years	Warm, natural look, very durable, doesn't show fingerprints, now very affordable	Satin nickel has gotten almost *too* popular. It's no longer the unique look it once was.
Polished nickel	An up-and-comer, a warmer alternative to polished chrome	Shows fingerprints and smudges
Oil-rubbed bronze: An up-and-coming look	A dramatic, pretty look that works beautifully with antique looks	Bronze tones vary more from manufacturer to manufacturer than nickels do, so it's harder to match the faucet to other hardware
Wrought iron	Similar to oil-rubbed bronze but a colder tone	Pricey
Stainless steel	Matches steel sink	Again, watch out for that autopsy-room, too-much-steel look!
PVD coating: The new miracle material, PVD coating gets a gold star for its ability to prevent tarnishing	Extremely durable and long lasting, it's available in dozens of finishes, like pewter, iron, bronze, copper, gold, and more	Pricey

■ **Do you want all the water that comes out of your faucet to be filtered, or just some?** Do you want a separate faucet for filtered water, or a one-faucet system that allows you to switch between filtered and nonfiltered water?

■ **What level of filtration do you want?** Some basic systems have a carbon-based filter to take out chlorine and lead, and make the water taste better. Or more advanced filtering systems will also help put the whammy on viruses, parasitic cysts, bacteria, and the like.

■ **Filtration system built into the faucet spray head, or a separate filtration canister under the sink?** If you want a lot of filtered water, the under-counter systems are more cost-effective. You can also use any style faucet you want on top. You don't have to get the filtration system and the faucet from the same company.

Some potential problems:

■ **Ask your filtration system dealer about water pressure.** Filtering water will tend to lower the pressure. Make sure you're getting enough flow.

■ **Consider the expense and hassle of replacing the filters.** Make sure you get a system

where the directions on how to replace the filter aren't a thirty-two-page booklet. And figure out how much a gallon of filtered water costs, based on the cost of the filters. If the filter is expensive and doesn't last that long, your built-in may not give you the savings over bottled water you'd hoped for.

■ **Consider the expense of the system.** The larger systems, where every drop of water in your whole house is being filtered, are not cheap. Still, when you compare it to waking up one morning with your whole family sporting a vaguely luminescent green tint because some of some malevolent microbes in the water supply, it may well be worth the cost.

Floor It

Flooring is another area that has improved in terms of products that both look great and are highly functional. Consider how much traffic and abuse the thing gets. Then think carefully before getting something that's gorgeous but has maintenance issues—unless, of course, you're not the one who will be cleaning it.

Some flooring issues to consider:

■ **Vinyl and linoleum: not the same thing.** Linoleum has been around since the early

FLOORING AT A GLANCE		
MATERIAL	**PROS**	**CONS**
Limestone and slate: Great for Contemporary and Zen looks, elegant and durable	A natural matte look that can be carried over onto a backsplash. It's affordably priced, and comes in a variety of choices.	Must be sealed properly, and resealed periodically. Stone can be cold, and the hard surface can be difficult to stand on for long periods.
Ceramic tile: One of the oldest flooring materials, great for Mediterranean, Southwest, and other classic looks	Ceramic tile is extremely durable, and comes in a wide range of colors and looks, from formal to rustic-looking, dramatic, and glamorous	Tile surfaces with grout are always harder to clean than a smooth surface and can be difficult to stand on
Linoleum: A classic floor material that's made a comeback in recent years, great for retro and vintage looks.	Long wearing, since the patterns go all the way through the material. It is also sanitary and affordable; made of all-natural ingredients that make it a "green" choice.	Linoleum is more porous than vinyl, so it must be cared for with floor wax. It can be tricky to install, as well.
Vinyl: The basic floor choice, great for Contemporary or Modern Retro	Probably the most affordable flooring material on the market. Vinyl is low maintenance and easy to install. It also comes in a wide array of colors and patterns.	Vinyl is not as long lasting as linoleum. Additionally, vinyl that's designed to simulate other materials often looks fake.
Laminate: You can have a beautiful wood floor look without the maintenance issues	It's easy to clean and softer than stone or ceramic tile, thus easier to stand on. Amtico's line of "wood" floors (also come with cool inlay options) and BHK's wood-look laminates provide great, authentic wood looks.	Wood-look laminate can be as expensive as real wood, yet it sometimes looks fake. It also can warp if exposed to water for long periods.
Hardwood: Real wood can make a truly elegant design statement. If you have a great room arrangement, you can bring hardwood into your kitchen for a consistent floor throughout.	Hardwood is beautiful, and is increasingly affordable, with many prefinished systems perfect for DIY projects.	Must be sealed, requires a fair amount of maintenance; scratches easily and is not ideal if you have pets. Wood floors can also warp if exposed to water for long periods. Be careful when buying wood, make sure it's solid, not engineered wood.

FLOORING AT A GLANCE

MATERIAL	PROS	CONS
Concrete: If you have a large space and are going for an open, loft/industrial look, this is a trendy choice that gives you a striking look	It's as durable as stone and tile, but less expensive in some fabrications. It can be buffed to a very glossy shine, and dyed different colors. Precast concrete can also be made to effectively mimic limestone for far less money.	Can be very cold in the winter. A porous substance; needs to be sealed, or it will stain. A messy installation. The hard surface can also be hard on the legs. Also, mind your total concrete space, and avoid the underground bunker look.

Your kitchen floor needs to be highly functional. Here, some snappy-looking choices meant for the garage, but also great for Urban Industrial and other Contemporary looks. **PHOTO:** *Courtesy of Gladiator* ▷

1900s and is an authentic pick for twentieth-century design. Vinyl came around in the late 1940s, so it's good for Modern Retro or Contemporary looks, not period themes.

WARNING: If you're restoring an old house that has ancient (before 1971) linoleum, the existing underlayment could have asbestos in it. While it's not doing you any damage attached to the floor, removing it can cause asbestos fibers to become airborne and cause a possible health hazard. If this is the case with your restoration project, *you have to find out the proper procedures for removing asbestos,* a subject beyond the scope of this book.

- **Is concrete possible in your space?** The concrete floor is usually something that's installed in new construction. Cast-in-place concrete (as opposed to precast concrete, which is what fabricators do for countertops) is a very messy job. Wet concrete is also very heavy, so putting a layer of fresh concrete on an existing floor may not be a feasible solution in all instances. For more information about concrete: www.decorativeconcreteinstitute.com

- **Warm it up.** A floor heating system will add a wonderfully luxurious touch—especially if you live in a cold climate and are opting for stone or ceramic tile. Heating cables, which must be embedded in

Stone makes for a beautifully classic floor. **PHOTO:** *Courtesy of The Craft-Art Company, Inc.* ◀

Good old linoleum is back— it's considered a more "green" product than vinyl tile, and a cool retro look, such as this bright Marmoleum floor from Forbo. **PHOTO:** *Courtesy of Forbo* ▶

cementatious material under the tile or stone, are relatively easy to install. However, this does add an extra step in your flooring installation, and an extra expense.

RESOURCES: www.ifloor.com has an amazing array of floor products to help you zero in on what you're looking for.

Paradise by the Kitchen Light

Remember when kitchen lighting consisted of one ugly central overhead fixture that had the unfortunate tendency to collect the little bitty corpses of dead flies? And then, those boxy fluorescent fixtures came on the market and gave everything a sickly greenish tint.

No other part of kitchen design has improved as much as lighting. Today's lights use the principles of theatrical and film lighting to help make your kitchen the showplace it is.

TYPES OF LIGHTING

There are three types of lighting: **general, task,** and **accent.** Lighting is usually either **decorative** or **functional,** and you want a mix of both kinds. You also want your lights to be on different "zone" circuits, with different switches so you can create ambience. For instance, a pretty,

atmospheric look is perfect for dinnertime, while brighter lights are better for cooking. Putting dimmers on your lights will give you even more lighting options.

WARNING: The more complex your lighting system gets, the more you need real knowledge of electrical wiring to pull it off. If this is not your specialty, do yourself a favor and hire a

Wood-look floors have greatly improved in recent years. Here, Tarkett's comfortable, low-maintenance FiberFloor.

PHOTO: *Courtesy of Tarkett* ▲

Today's wide array of lighting options can help to make your kitchen a true showplace. DESIGNER: *Gary White, CMKBD, CID (Kitchen & Bath Design)* PHOTO: *Larry Falke* ▼

professional. Lighting designers charge a lot of money to install complicated automated lighting systems, and there's a reason for that. Incorrectly installed electrical work can kill someone or burn down your house. Or it can just continually malfunction and drive you crazy. Again, just because you've spent the last decade watching *This Old House* does *not* mean you are qualified to do your own electrical work.

■ **General lighting** creates an overall ambience, providing diffused lighting for moving around the room without tripping over chairs. Those ugly overheads of yesteryear were "general" lighting. These days, general lighting is likely to be something more attractive, like recessed lighting. Recessed downlights, which provide a row of spotlights, is a current trend.

A good time to plan lighting is when you're making alterations to the ceiling. If, for instance, you're altering ceiling heights to denote the passage from kitchen to home entertainment room in a great room arrangement, this is an opportunity to put in recessed lighting or other effects. ■

- **Task lighting** illuminates a particular area where tasks are performed, such as the food prep station on an island. The lighting that comes with your vent hood, and illuminates your cooktop, is another example of task lighting.

- **Accent lighting** generally spotlights a design element, such as a piece of art on

Lighting controls have gotten much more advanced in recent years, with all kinds of complex automated lighting systems available. These include motion-detection lights and "smart" lighting that you can access remotely, or program for timed settings at different times of the day. ■

the wall. Lighting around cabinets is another example of accent lighting.

WARNING: Make sure recessed downlights in the ceiling are properly installed. Otherwise, water vapor from cooking can travel through the air and through a recessed fixture, and get into the attic or wall cavity, leading to mold and mildew. This is especially a problem with cathedral ceilings.

WHERE TO BEGIN?

Start planning with the **task lights.** You'll want these over the cooktop, in food prep areas, and under cabinets to light up the countertops. Then, add general and accent lighting.

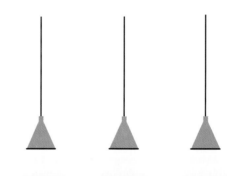

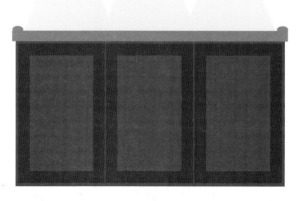

The beam spread from three pendant lights illuminates a wide area. ◀

Multiple pendant lights over an island make for a beautiful lighting scheme. **DESIGNER:** *Brice Zickuhr, AIA (Metropolitan Designs)* **PHOTO:** *Richard Sprengler* ▶

When using lighting in groups, position it so it illuminates all of your target area. Lighting designers track a light's beam spread, where the light will spill to. ▪

ALL LIT UP

There are three basic kinds of lighting fixtures: **incandescent, fluorescent,** and **halogen.** A mix of all three will give your kitchen a pretty, artful look.

- **Incandescent** lights are your regular light-bulb type. They generate the most heat, and also burn out the most quickly, but they have an attractive, warm feel.

When planning your lighting, don't forget the computer station. Your computer itself will be lit, but you'll need to illuminate the desk space with a task light. This can be a fairly small light, like a table lamp. Remember, too much light will make it hard to see your computer screen. ▪

- **Halogen** lights are great for lighting spaces above and below the cabinets. You can use miniature track lights or low-voltage linear systems to illuminate countertops and put accent lights on the ceiling.

- **Fluorescent** lighting is the most energy efficient and long lasting. The good news is that it's improved in recent years, so it doesn't have to be ugly anymore. Old fluorescent bulbs had uncontrolled color temperature. Color of light depends on the phosphor coatings inside, and this is something lamp manufacturers traditionally didn't focus on. But now, you can buy fluorescents with rare

A decorative lighting fixture can create a beautiful focal point that exemplifies the design style of the room.
DESIGNER: *Leslie Cohen, CKD, ASID (Leslie Cohen Designs)* ▼

In some states, you *must* use fluorescent lights in your kitchen remodel. For instance, California's Title 24 mandates that kitchens and baths must be primarily lit by fluorescent light, and that light must be activated by the first switch upon entering the room. ■

earth phosphors. These lights are more expensive, but give you a warmer light that's similar to incandescent bulbs.

When planning your fluorescent lighting, make sure the beam of light bounces off the ceiling or other surface, rather than shining directly in people's eyes. For instance, you could put fluorescents on top of crown moldings, or up inside a coffer.

■ **Lighting styles** are now available in an amazing variety of looks and finishes. Just like your faucet, your lighting can be a wonderful, relatively inexpensive way of reinforcing your kitchen's theme. So splurge on a top-quality light fixture that exemplifies your specific design style.

So there you have it. Hopefully, you're not overwhelmed, but instead have armed yourself with a basic plan to narrow down your choices to some styles, products, finishes, and add-ons that appeal to you. Make some notes, or take this chapter with you for a couple of window shopping trips to a local kitchen dealership or home center. That way, you can take a look at your preliminary choices up close and personal.

Once you decide on products, you'll be ready to take the plunge and put your kitchen plan in action.

CHAPTER 8

THE INSTALLMENT PLAN

This is the moment when the kitchen of your dreams, the kitchen portrayed in that lovely computer graphic your designer gave you, is going to become an actual room that you can hang out in.

Sadly, this is also the point where a lot of projects go awry. What can go wrong in a $75,000 kitchen is sometimes different than the disaster that can befall a $10,000 remodel, but rest assured, there's enough nail-biting, screaming, and threats of legal action available for everyone.

People seem to have countless horror stories about installations. Some of these stories are, unfortunately, true (though some may be dramatized a tad to give them more punch as a Thanksgiving dinner anecdote).

But it doesn't have to be that way! With a little patience and some careful planning, you can help to ensure that your remodeling story has a happy ending. Here are some things to keep in mind.

Finding an Installer Who Won't Give You a Nervous Breakdown

Face it, hiring people and entrusting them to alter expensive stuff that you're very attached to is nerve-wracking. And this is, after all, *your house*. You're going to be really upset if those $30,000 cabinets warp because they were installed just a tiny bit unevenly. So don't make the mistake of hiring a kitchen installer strictly because he quoted you the lowest price. Look for the right person, rather than the right price.

There are several ways to approach the installation process.

Design/Build: For a high-end kitchen, you might not have to go through the process of finding an installer at all. Your installer will be the guy parking his big shiny truck right next to your designer's BMW. They work for the same company as part of a design/build team that takes care of your project from beginning to end. They may subcontract plumbing and electrical work, but they will take care of finding these people for you.

Many of the best designers and architects prefer design/build for one simple reason: They have control of the project—they deal with the headaches and reap the rewards. It's a streamlined system that ensures that the designer's

A design/build approach will enable designers to best bring their vision to your project, since everyone works for the same team. **DESIGNER:** *Bruce Zickuhr, AIA (Metropolitan Designs)* **PHOTO:** *Richard Sprengler* ▼

It's the details that make or break a project. Here, neutral tones and a clean-lined storage island with cooktop equal a great-looking, highly functional kitchen. PHOTO: *Courtesy of CaesarStone* ▲

vision will translate to an actual, real-life kitchen. This also simplifies *your* life, because if a problem occurs, you now get one go-to person to rely on, instead of a group of people all blaming the other guy. If you have a generous budget and want to minimize your stress levels, this is definitely the way to go.

Design/Build Lite: Unfortunately, many terrific designers don't do their own installations. In fact, many designers these days are going independent, with no showroom.

However, these designers will still commandeer the project through the installation process for you if you'll let them. Practically all high-end designers have a handful of contractors they like to work with. Contractually, you, as the homeowner, hire the contractor separately, but this is your designer's guy. He's already done thirty-seven other kitchens with your designer, and they know how to work together. If your cabinets cost more than your car, don't try to save some money by having your Uncle Fred install them, even if he did do a perfectly good job with that tiki bar he built on his patio.

Don't hire the installer who undercuts the guy your designer recommends by $1,000, either. Your designer, a smart professional that *you* picked, made a huge effort to find good contractors and establish relationships with them. Your designer's research methods and contacts in the industry are far better than yours. Some designers make their clients sign a waiver saying, if you don't use their recommended contractor, they're not liable for any unfortunate results. You might take that as a hint.

Buy It Yourself: Maybe you're planning to do your own design, and buy products from a home center. Do you have to use their installer? No. He may or may not be just fine. Before you sign your life, and your really amazing, personally picked-out Shaker cabinets, away, do some research.

Overall, the best way to find an installer is by referral and word of mouth. Have any family or friends remodeled recently? If so, did they have a pleasant experience? Ask other tradespeople, as well, because good people in the business know other good people. Maybe the person who did such a super job with your landscaping knows someone who installs kitchens.

If you don't know anyone personally, the National Association of the Remodeling Industry (www.nari.org) can refer you to a certified remodeler in your area. Only full-time, professional remodeling contractors are eligible for certification by NARI. The screening process to receive such a certification is intense. It requires proof of hands-on experience, industry training, involvement in continuing education, technical skills, practices in business management, as well as association and community service. This should give you some level of confidence that you're dealing with a professional.

The Internet also offers several contractor referral services such as HandyMan.com and ImproveNet.com. These services offer a roster of contractors prescreened to weed out any fly-by-night guys. They check a contractor's credit, business, and legal history, as well as licensing, and are typically free to consumers.

If you decide to go with someone not recommended to you, check them out thoroughly. Call the Better Business Bureau and Consumer Affairs. See if there are complaints on file, and how they were resolved. Call the installer's references and talk to them for a while. Check to see if their license is up-to-date, and if they've ever been sued.

Remember, anybody doing business can get the occasional insane client who regards suing people as a fun and exciting hobby. So, one lawsuit doesn't automatically mean your potential installer is a crook. However, if a whole bunch of people are going the courtroom route with the guy, run, do not walk, to the nearest exit.

For a major project, try to meet your installer in person before signing on the dotted line. Make sure you feel comfortable with him or her. Your installer will be traipsing through your house for days, weeks, or even months, and it will be easier all around if you like each other.

If you are going with a contractor who is not referred to you by friends or your designer, try to see his or her *actual work*, not just photos on a Web site. It's the details that really make or break a job, and a photo won't show that splotch of wood filler on the wall that sits under the paint, or the place where the refrigerator panel scrapes the wall. So ask if you can go see a previous project in person.

ASK A BETTER QUESTION

Here are some things to ask your potential installer:

- How long have you been in business?

- How many jobs do you do a year?

- How many employees do you have?

- Which portions of a job do you subcontract out? If you subcontract parts of the job, will I be able to meet the subcontractors first? Will you be on-site to supervise them?

- Are you licensed, bonded, and insured, and are all of these up-to-date? Can I see the paperwork for this?

- How do you handle problems? For instance, if I think something looks uneven and the worker thinks it looks fine, what happens next?

- What is your track record for timely job completion?

- How much experience do you have with the products I've chosen? All lines of cabinetry have their own special quirks, so if a cabinet installer hasn't installed a certain brand of cabinets before, it could be problematic. If you're finding your own installer, you can call the product manufacturer for a list of factory-licensed installers in your area.

WARNING: Some products that have a warranty are *not* warranteed if you don't have them installed by someone factory certified by the manufacturer. If that's the case, definitely go with the factory-certified installer for that segment of your remodel, even if he's more expensive than your overall contractor.

THE BOY SCOUTS WERE RIGHT

"Be Prepared" is indeed a good motto. The best kind of problem is the kind you prevent in the first place, so here are some steps to bring you closer to an angst-free installation day.

- **Get it in writing.** Once you've decided on your installer, make sure you get a complete estimate—in writing. Some people charge extra to tear out your old cabinets; others will charge extra for the Dumpster. Get it in writing who is responsible and who is paying for any problems that might arise after the fact. These might include leaky plumbing, cabinet doors that stick, or flooring that has bubbles or uneven spots.

- **Understand the timetable.** Talk to your installer in advance about what kind of schedule works best for everyone involved.

Installers tend to start early in the morning to maximize daylight hours, so if you're a night owl who likes to sleep in, having a hammer banging away at six a.m. will be just one more added stress in an already stressful situation. If your installer is flexible, you may be able to compromise on the start time. If this isn't possible, begin adjusting your schedule at least a week prior to the start date of the job to help your body adapt. This way, you're not starting the installation process overtired and cranky.

Prepare your house. Think about how you're going to perform necessary kitchen functions during the installation process. Because guess what you're not going to have while they're remodeling your kitchen? Running water, access to the refrigerator, and cooking capabilities. The laundry room—which also has running water so you can wash dishes—can serve as a temporary kitchen. Beg, borrow, or steal a little office refrigerator, move your microwave and coffeemaker in there, and keep your temporary kitchen stocked with the basics for the duration. Being able to have coffee and an English muffin in the morning will help keep you grounded during the remodeling process. It may also help alleviate that feeling that your home has turned into a postapocalyptic alien planet.

Remember, too, that dust from the work in the kitchen will creep into other areas of your house. Dust is sneaky like that. Make sure you cover upholstery, other flooring, pet dishes, and the like, and make sure the workers seal off the remodel area as much as possible. Try to keep all the doors in the house closed. If you have allergies, this might be a good time to get yourself an air filter and stock up on your medication.

CREATURE COMFORTS: Your critters need to be taken care of during this process, too. Keep your dog or cat in a different part of the house than the work area. And make sure the installers know where this is, so they don't accidentally let Cujo out—or get bitten by your grumpy, overly protective pet. Also, make sure dust, toxic fumes, cold wind, or other health-threatening invasives are kept far away from your parrot or reptile's cage, and out of your aquarium water.

ONCE YOUR INSTALLER IS ON THE JOB

Even if your installer seems to be on the ball, don't assume everything is fine. Don't hover over the workers, but don't blithely go about your business and assume that everything's going to be fine, either. While you don't want to get in the way, do keep your eyes open for signs of trouble.

Keep alert so you can monitor any of the following bad signs—should they occur.

BAD SIGN #1: How long does your contractor say it will take to install your kitchen? Some zip through the entire thing in two days; while high-end installers sometimes take a week to just put in the cabinets. Faster is not necessarily better, so if your contractor is rushing through the process at breakneck speed, he may not be taking care of the details.

BAD SIGN #2: Overall sloppiness. The workers should be cleaning up at the end of the day—every day. Installation means plenty of dust, dirt, and general messiness. A lot of this can't be helped, but a good installer will make sure everything is left as tidy as possible. Convey your expectations about this in advance.

BAD SIGN #3: Their schedule changes often, and you don't know about it. A well-managed project is planned ahead of time. The contractor should tell you when things have changed—and not six hours after he was supposed to have arrived at your house. Clear communication is at the center of every successful job.

YOUR DESIGNER'S PART

If you have a professional designer, that person should be there at the beginning of every major phase of installation to make sure everything is on track. Once the installation is in progress, it becomes more expensive to fix things that were done incorrectly because the installer couldn't read the designer's plans. For instance, the day the cabinets arrive, your designer should check the shipment to confirm sizes and details.

Your designer should also be ready and willing to discuss your concerns with the contractor, especially if it's a contractor the designer recommended. For example, if you feel like the guy is doing a slipshod job installing the cabinets, this is something you should tell the designer immediately.

How to Deal with Your Installer So You Won't Give Him a Nervous Breakdown

For every complaint that homeowners have about contractors, contractors have a gripe about their customers: Those flaky homeowners always change their minds. They forget to leave the keys. They don't pay on time. They hover over you like a giant paranoid bee and drive you crazy. Their Rottweiler is sitting just outside the work area eyeing your lunch.

Remember, making the installation process a pleasant experience requires good behavior from the homeowner as well as the contractor.

TIPS TO KEEP YOUR INSTALLER OFF PAXIL

You went to a lot of trouble to find a top-quality installer. But even good installers, like milk left out on the table, can turn sour if you don't follow a few basic rules.

No deadline pressure. Yes, it would be lovely to have your kitchen done in time for Thanksgiving, or your daughter's graduation. But is it a good idea to get your kitchen remodeled with a set-in-stone deadline? *No!* Why? Things can go wrong. The truck carrying your granite countertop can get sideswiped, causing a giant crack that means the top has to be refabricated. And then when it finally gets there, the contractor can't install it that week because he's committed to another job. Having a hard deadline puts needless stress on everybody involved in the process.

Stay out of the kitchen. Let them do their work. You went through that whole decision-making process, and now it's the installer's time to do his job. So let him do it.

Don't change your mind. Deciding you want a triple-bowl sink instead of the double-bowl one you picked may mean fabricating—and paying for—a whole new top. However, smaller changes in midstream can set a project off-kilter, too. They can delay the job, annoy your installer, and set off a snowball effect of problems. Once you've got your plan, stick to it.

A little knowledge is a dangerous thing. Regular viewing of *This Old House* and *Trading Spaces* does not make you an expert on remodeling. Don't give your installer any tips; don't touch his tools or try to help him in any way.

Accept Murphy's law. Sometimes, a little thing can go wrong and it's nobody's fault; sometimes a huge thing can go wrong and it's nobody's fault, either. You didn't know there were termites behind your old cabinets before you took them out. But there they are—this changes the job, and you have to deal with it. Stay calm, and remember the old adage, "Focus 20 percent on the problem and 80 percent on the solution."

Give them access. They can't remodel your kitchen if they can't get into your kitchen. They need your cell phone number, and you need theirs—and you need to coordinate your schedules. If you work full time, or will be out while the work is being done, they will also need your security system code so they can lock up after they're done working. This is one of the reasons why it's important to hire a bonded, licensed contractor you can trust.

Finally, remember to breathe. Installation is generally the most difficult part of a remodeling job. But it also means you're closing in on

Clear communication is essential for accomplishing a successful job such as this one. DESIGNER: *Gary White, CMKBD, CID (Kitchen & Bath Design)* PHOTO: *Larry Falke* ▶

the end product—the kitchen of your dreams. So use this time to catch up with family and friends (preferably those with working kitchens who might take pity on you and invite you for dinner). And don't be afraid to take advantage of their hospitality. After all, before long, you'll be planning your own dinner parties, so you can show off your brand-new kitchen!

CHAPTER 9

THE MORNING AFTER

Dealing with Problems After the Fact

One of the great truisms of home remodeling projects is that no matter how careful you are, things still can go wrong.

The glass topping your cooktop inexplicably shatters a week after the job is done. Or the instant hot water dispenser dispenses water that tastes more like molten copper than actual water. Or perhaps the cabinet panel on the dishwasher has a funny blue streak in it that doesn't match the rest of the cabinetry.

So, how do you protect yourself against things that go wrong? Like the cyber romance that seemed like such a great idea until you met him in person, most problems that occur after the fact can be avoided if you start with a little preventive medicine.

One of the best things you can do to protect yourself against future problems is to keep all product warranties and paperwork in order. Keeping track of your records can save you major headaches later on.

Dealing with well-known brand-name companies can also pay dividends if there are problems later on. In general, the higher profile a company has, the less it's going to want to risk damage to its reputation. If you work through a kitchen dealership, ask them which manufacturers are most customer-friendly should problems arise. They deal with kitchen products all the time, so they know the inside scoop.

Write the date and year on all warranties, product manuals, and product paperwork. Then, file all of them in a binder, and put them away for safekeeping. Keeping orderly records not only protects you if there are problems down the road, it can also help you when it comes time to sell your house. Potential buyers will not only be impressed by your organizational skills, they will also believe that you're the kind of person who maintains your home—a big plus if they're thinking of buying it. ■

If you're doing the project solo, ask people you know. Surely someone has a story about an appliance that broke four times in the first six months and can tell you whether the manufacturer stepped up to the plate or suddenly went MIA.

Additionally, keep in mind that companies that have been in business for fifty years are a good bet to be around ten years from now when you have a problem. Sometimes, it's worth a few extra dollars to have the security of knowing there will be someone to complain to if things go wrong.

Conversely, beware of buying products from companies that have been in business only a short time. Even a great warranty is useless if the company goes bankrupt a year or two down the road.

It's also a good idea to check return policies before you buy something. This way, if the built-in knife rack doesn't fit where you thought it would, or the plumbing for the new sink takes up too much space to allow room for that nifty recycling unit you thought you needed, you're not stuck with them.

But what happens if you did everything right, and things still go wrong?

How to Complain Effectively and Get Results!

Okay, so maybe you don't know everything about cabinets, and work triangles make you dizzy. But complaints—this is something you don't need a book for! After all, you might think, "How can I not be good at complaining? I complain all the time."

But the fact is, complaining successfully, like anything else, takes practice, skill, and a certain amount of people savvy. It's part science, part art, and part timing. The squeaky wheel may get the grease, but if it's *too* squeaky, it may get the whole cart tossed out with the trash.

So, how do you go about complaining effectively? First, figure out what you want to accomplish—then plan your strategy. You may think you have a valid complaint, and you may well be right. But the first rule of thumb is that it's not just what you say, but who you say it to, when you say it, and how.

TALK TO THE RIGHT PERSON

Addressing complaints to the wrong people is not only a waste of time, but it can also get you branded a troublemaker before you even begin to make your case. Ideally, you want to be able to sit down with the person who can help you and have a rational conversation. So, save your wrath for the person who deserves it—and make it a point to treat everyone else courteously.

TIME IT RIGHT

Likewise, when it comes to complaining effectively, timing is also essential. Walking into a company at closing time when everyone is tired, cranky, and ready to head home is *not* the best time to lodge a complaint.

If your goal is to get positive results, think about when you're most likely to find a receptive audience. As a rule, early in the day (but not too early) is a good place to start.

If you feel you're going to need more than a few minutes, and you want to get the person's full attention without suffering a million interruptions, make an appointment. Keep it simple. Explain that you'd like to request an appointment to discuss some concerns, and save the heavy artillery for the actual meeting.

Dress professionally; you don't need a suit, but a professional appearance is more convincing than jeans and a sweatshirt. It also shows that you are taking this seriously—and they should, too.

Bring along your notes. If it's written down on paper, you're less likely to forget something in the heat of the moment. Above all, remember that you're looking to enlist someone's assistance, even if that someone is the cause of your problem. So do everything in your power to make it easy for them to help you. Know the specifics of the problem—dates, times, make, and model numbers—and be able to convey this information without yelling, sarcasm, tears, or hysteria. By handling the situation calmly and rationally, you're more likely to be taken seriously and get the results you want.

CHOOSE HONEY OVER VINEGAR

Finally, the old adage about choosing honey over vinegar still holds true. Storming into someone's place of business and telling them they're an idiot, liar, or cheat may make *you* feel better, but it's not going to get your problem fixed. Even if the person *is* an idiot, a liar, or a cheat, saying so will only make them angry, and make you look like a crazy person.

Handle yourself with decorum and make your case firmly—but tactfully. Usually, when problems arise, both sides truly think they are right. But even if the other party knows they're wrong, and even if they deliberately attempted to rip you off, you may still be able to get the problem fixed if you can avoid backing them into a corner.

When arguing a specific issue, keep the following in mind:

- The vast majority of people are strongly motivated by self-interest. So, if you can show them that it will cause them more grief to fight you than to fix it, you're more likely to get the results you want.

- Don't start out by making threats. All this does is create an immediate chasm between you and the person whose help you need. As tempers rise, that chasm can quickly become impossible to breach. It's better to try to get both people on the same side, so everyone wins in the end. You can always save the threats for later.

- Don't harp on how unfair the situation is. Fewer people are motivated by a sense of fair play than you might think. You're generally better off arguing facts rather than principles.

- Be able to state in a calm, unemotional way what the problem is, how it came to be, why you feel the other party is responsible, and what, specifically, you want them to do to solve the problem.

- Hear the other person out with an open mind. There may be issues here that you truly don't understand, and listening may help you come up with possible solutions that will make both parties happy.

- Make sure you understand the other person's side by repeating back to them what you believe they said. This will show that you're listening and rational, and will help you to be sure you fully comprehend the situation. It can also prevent the situation from escalating out of control.

- Remember, a little flattery never hurt anyone. Begin with something positive that shows you expect that your problem will be addressed to your satisfaction. For instance, "I know ABC Kitchens has been around for more than fifty years, and I'd always heard that your company cares about quality work and customer service. That's why I felt confident doing business with you. So, when I had a problem, I felt I should come to you directly so we could get this resolved quickly." Don't underestimate the power of positive thinking. If you walk in convinced that they are going to help you, they may well follow your lead.

CALLS, E-MAILS, AND OTHER MISTAKES

Okay, you're angry, and you want to let someone have it. So you pick up the phone, call the company, and give the person on the other end a piece of your mind. You may feel better, but you've just made your situation worse. Here's why:

1. People find it easier to be rude or nasty when they're not face-to-face with you. Calling them on the phone makes it easy for them to blow you off, and takes away your best weapon, the face-to-face conversation.

2. Once you tell someone off, it's a lot harder to convince them to help you with your problem. Even if they know you're right, they may continue to fight just to save face.

3. If the entire exchange happens by phone only, there's no record of the conversation. That means if you end up in court, it turns into a he said/she said thing, which is useless in proving your case. Getting it in writing gives you more leverage.

4. Half the time, you get the wrong person on the phone and end up yelling at someone who has nothing to do with the problem. Now you've alienated yet another person who might have been able to help you.

If you're from the computer generation, you may see e-mail as a good way to make your point. Unfortunately, it rarely is. For one thing, e-mail is easy to delete, ignore, or scan through quickly and then forget about. The computer culture has evolved in such a way that e-mail is viewed primarily as a casual medium, so it rarely carries the weight of a more formal communiqué.

E-mail also can bring out the worst in people. While behavioral psychologists are still pondering the reasons, many people will say nasty things in e-mail that they would never say in person, or even in a written (hard copy) letter. Since your goal is to resolve a problem, not create an all-out war, avoid any medium that encourages people to behave badly.

Finally, e-mail simply doesn't have the same power and presentation as a formal letter of inquiry. It's fine for informal communications, but if you're serious about your complaint, don't relegate it to e-mail.

LETTERS OF COMPLAINT

So you've tried honey, vinegar, and threats to move your family of six into their kitchen until yours works properly. However, you've still gotten no results. Fortunately, there are places you can go to get some satisfaction.

THE BETTER BUSINESS BUREAU

The Better Business Bureau is a national organization that tracks positive and negative feedback about businesses. This includes records of any complaints, and how these were resolved. If you've been doing your homework, you checked out the people you were doing business with to see if they had a clean record *before* you began the project.

Unfortunately for you, they *did* have a clean record. But just your luck, everyone has a first mistake (or a first time for getting caught) and you're that unlucky first.

Filing a complaint with the Better Business Bureau will help warn future customers about your experiences with this company. Additionally, the Better Business Bureau may try to mediate the complaint for you. However, even if the Better Business Bureau is convinced that you have a valid complaint, you should be aware that this agency does not have the power to mandate compliance. So, while filing a complaint here is a good place to start, it may not be enough to get you the results you need.

CONSUMER AFFAIRS

Your local Consumer Affairs office has more teeth than the Better Business Bureau. If this agency finds evidence of fraudulent, illegal, or dishonest business practices, it can suspend a contractor's license. For this reason, a carefully constructed letter outlining the problem, your attempts to resolve it, and the company's response (or lack thereof) can be quite effective.

If you feel the company's behavior was not just unethical but illegal, you may also want to send a note to the state Attorney General's office. In fact, if you want real results, write a carefully constructed letter detailing the problem, when it occurred, why you believe the company is responsible, and what outcome you are looking for. No personal attacks, just the facts. Then, copy the letter to the Better Business Bureau, Consumer Affairs, the Attorney General's office, and the company itself (so they know that you're serious enough about this to take action).

Many companies will ignore complaints if they think they can get away with it. After all, when most people feel ripped off, they will complain to friends, relatives, and the company itself, but will eventually let it go. In fact, some shady companies count on this fact. But once they realize you're serious about this—and not going to walk away that readily—they're more likely to try to resolve the issue.

As a last resort, you can contact one of the TV "watchdog" shows that handles consumer complaints. No one likes bad publicity, and sometimes the threat of a public complaint will be enough to get results when nothing else has worked.

Tip

Whatever you do, don't refuse payment and just ignore the situation. The longer a situation drags on, the more likely it is to lead to expensive legal hassles, or even a mechanic's lien on your house. ■

After-the-Fact Fixes

While there are certainly problems that can require expensive fixes and more visits from your contractor, you may be able to address

Your lighting scheme will affect how colors are perceived in your kitchen space. Here, innovative lighting plays counterpoint with cool Element aluminum and glass doors. PHOTO: *Courtesy of Element* ▶

some seemingly major problems without breaking the bank—or your remodeler's neck.

Consider the following scenarios:

1. The cabinets with that slightly pinkish tint looked great at Home Depot. In your kitchen, however, they look frighteningly like Attack of the Bubble Yum Creatures. You try to tell yourself it's just your imagination. But when everyone who views them leaves humming the theme from the *Pink Panther*, you know you're in trouble. Don't panic, there is always a solution.

One of the most common complaints

in kitchen design is that products look different out of the store or showroom, and sometimes the color difference is dramatic. So, what happened? Did the cabinet company manufacture one beige cabinet display and then create 14,953 others that some-how ended up bubble-gum pink by accident? Probably not. Perhaps the lighting in the showroom simply made the cabinets look paler, while the lighting in your kitchen brings out the pink undertones.

Fortunately, if the problem is color

related, you may just have to adjust the lighting. Something as simple as changing the type of lightbulb can avert a crisis.

First, look at your colors and figure out whether they are warm or cool, then make sure your light is complementary.

As a rule, using cool light will intensify cool colors, while using warm or yellow-orange light will intensify warm colors and wash out cool colors. Neutral light will affect neither.

If you run out of tile and the pattern is discontinued, try mixing and matching different tiles. This not only solves the problem, it also allows you to add a unique personal touch. PHOTO: *Courtesy of Walker Zanger* ◂

2. You thought you had enough tile to finish the backsplash, but somehow you've run short. Unfortunately, your tile selection has been discontinued. You've been to every tile place in the city and no one has any leftovers.

Depending on how short you've run, you may be able to hide the problem by using the same-sized tile with a different pattern in places that would be hidden, such as behind the range top or ventilation unit.

If you're still short, buy same-sized tiles in a complementary color and create a border around the edges. It will look like you deliberately did this to personalize the design.

3. When the original measurements were taken for the refrigerator, it fit just fine in the space allotted for it. However, the custom panel added just enough extra depth that now, every time you open the refrigerator door, it scrapes the paint off the wall.

First, try pulling the refrigerator out another inch or two. The extra inch shouldn't make the appliance protrude noticeably, but may solve the scraping problem. If this doesn't work, you may be able to remove the custom panel and sand down the side facing the refrigerator to thin it out enough to ensure a better fit.

4. The cabinet doors are rough to the touch, and you can see what looks like little dots of finish across the front.

This is actually due to overspray, and it's an easy fix. Take a brown paper bag and run it over the surface of the cabinet. It takes the overspray right off, giving you the smooth finish you expected.

5. Storage was an issue for you, so you wanted cabinets all the way up to the ceiling. Unfortunately, the installer nixed using moldings because your ceiling height varies in several spots. Now you've got the cabinets installed up to the ceiling, but because of the slight height variation, there are gaps in some places between the cabinets and the ceiling and it looks awful.

Don't get upset—just pick up a little caulk in a color that matches the cabinets, and fill in the gaps. Voilà—everything looks clean and perfect again.

Color accents in an unexpected place can brighten up a monochromatic kitchen. **DESIGNER:** *John Sofio (Built, Inc.)* **PHOTO:** *Courtesy of Lone Pine Pictures* ◀

6. The beautiful glass tile you picked out for the backsplash was an installer's nightmare. Several tiles are cracked, and your installer says taking them out and replacing them will just cause others to crack due to the delicate nature of the material.

   If the damage is confined to one area, you may be able to hide it behind an appliance garage, knife rack, or other accessory. If the damage is extensive, you may want to crack more of them and go for a crackled effect. Or you could have a mural hand-painted on the tiles. This will not only draw the eye away from any imperfections, it also will give you a uniquely personalized element that can act as a focal point for the room.

7. You thought you wanted the clean monochromatic look, but now you feel like the whole room has a stark, rather sterile feel to it. Who knew white could be so unfriendly?

   Liven up the room with a piece of artwork, a shelf that showcases your favorite collectibles, or a few brightly colored accent pieces. Perhaps you can add a splash of color with a cobalt blue pitcher with bright yellow flowers, a hanging multicolored quilt, or some eye-catching fabric for the curtains.

   You can also soften a too-stark room by painting the walls a shade slightly darker than the rest of the room. Look for a neutral color that has warmer undertones to add depth.

8. Your roll-outs sound like your son's 1977 Buick, and getting your pull-outs to actually pull out is akin to a gym workout.

   Roll-outs and pull-outs should move in and out smoothly. Always have your installer check these before pronouncing the job done. However, even if he's long gone, you can usually adjust these easily with a screwdriver.

9. You wanted the oversized range and the giant sink, but you didn't realize how little counter space you'd end up with. Now you feel like there's no place to prepare food.

   Many companies make cutting boards that fit over the sink to add work space when you need it. There's also a wood-top product that can be fitted directly over the top of the range to turn it into extra workspace when it's not in use.

When All Else Fails

When all else fails, try a little creativity.

A home magazine recently showcased an eye-catching kitchen that featured beautifully distressed cabinetry. Ironically, the cabinetry didn't start out that way. Rather, the cabinets were severely scratched up during the installation process, and the installer—whose license was not up-to-date—left the country shortly after the job was completed. The manufacturer claimed no responsibility, blaming it on the installer. The installer was no longer accessible, and the homeowner was left holding the bag.

But a clever designer helped the homeowner salvage the situation by taking advantage of those scratches and "distressing" the rest of the cabinetry to match. The end result is a stunning kitchen that wins compliments from everyone who sees it.

Because, really, isn't design ultimately about creativity? Don't be afraid to let yours blossom!

CHAPTER 10

FINISHING TOUCHES

The installers are gone, the designer no longer calls you daily, and the trucks outside your home are a distant memory. Even better, your new kitchen looks amazing. The cabinets that you were only 98 percent sure about in the store turned out to be the perfect choice. The chocolate glaze picks up the softer hues of the granite countertops, while all those pull-outs and roll-outs make storage a cinch. And the lighting shows it all off to maximum effect.

Discovering Your Passion for Design

You finally have your dream kitchen. And we also hope you've learned to really appreciate good design. Maybe you've found a style that you truly love, which you want to research more and make an integral part of your home's overall design statement. Or maybe you've discovered a collectible that really resonates with you—and combing flea markets and swap meets for great vintage finds has become your new favorite hobby.

Creative Ideas for Accessorizing

You can also have fun with your remodel leftovers in accessorizing your new kitchen. For instance, do you absolutely love the 1"x1" tiles you picked out for the backsplash? Glue together some of the extra tile to make matching trivets. These are beautiful *and* useful.

Do you still have the samples of counter-top material you first got when you started shopping? The small squares can make wonderful coasters, while larger ones are perfect to place plants on. If you have several different squares in complementary colors, you can even lay out a whole herb garden on your windowsill (color code them, so you can remember which one is the basil and which is the bay leaf).

Plants are one of the easiest and least expensive ways to make your kitchen look good. Don't limit yourself to the planters available at the home center. Instead, look for unique and interesting containers to plant them in. Old copper pots and cookie tins are just two options with a "kitchen-y" feel. ■

You can also get creative with extra pieces of decorative hardware. These can be used to create an unusual napkin holder, or a place to hang keys.

Of course, you're not limited to leftover products from the remodel. If you find your no-nonsense, no-frills kitchen is just a bit *too* nonfrilly, a trip to the curtain store may be in order. Material can be used to soften the look of a room, add texture, give a burst of color, or create an interesting focal point. Look for

hanging quilts, soft, filmy curtains, or woven place mats to add material appeal. Or, go for a clean look and film noir-ish shadows with wooden blinds.

Perhaps you put in all those nifty open shelves for collectibles, forgetting that you haven't lived in your home long enough to collect anything except bills. Now is a great time to start a collection. If you have a period theme, look to vases, decorative plates, and knickknacks from that era to complement your vintage look. For a Contemporary kitchen, keep collectibles to a minimum. One larger clean-lined piece such as a sculpture or plain stone bowl works better than a group of objects. If you're on a budget, you can find wonderful treasures at garage sales, in thrift shops, or on eBay.

If you don't want to clutter up that gorgeous new refrigerator with photos, magnets, and messages, maybe there's a spot on the wall where you can hang a message board. Go with a plain cork board, or dress it up with material from a craft store. You can use dried flowers, ribbon, glass mosaic tile, or an interesting stenciled border to transform your message board into a beautiful and functional work of art. Now you can showcase photos and communicate with members of your family without creating clutter.

You can also use framed photos to add a personal touch. If you don't want to go the traditional family pictures route, what about photos of favorite places? That beautiful picture

Displayed objects can warm up a modern space, but use them sparingly to maintain an uncluttered look. **PHOTO:** *Courtesy of Gaggenau* ▶

you took when you visited Venice can add a bit of Italian flair to your kitchen. Perhaps you even brought back some decorative souvenirs from your trip that can be used to continue the theme. Or maybe you have a beautiful framed picture of New Orleans that would look perfect above the spice rack where you keep all those Cajun spices.

If cooking is your passion, create a mini-library of cookbooks on a shelf or in a desk area.

Think in terms of scents, too. If you have a green thumb, a window herb garden can bring in delicious aromas. If you can't keep Astroturf alive without calling in a landscaping service, scented candles are a pretty and great-smelling alternative.

Remember, when it comes to accessorizing, the idea is to bring in items that have meaning to you. So, think about what you love—your favorite colors, places, people, hobbies, and passions. You can use these to help personalize your kitchen and make it a place that you enjoy spending time in.

But what if you can't decide what you want your accessory theme to be? Many designers suggest putting in a little shelf over the window for decorative items. But there's no law that says you have to have the same look every day. If you don't want to commit to one look, you can use this shelf as a constantly changing display case where you can showcase a red-and-gold Chinese vase one week and a collection of green glass bottles the next. Changing out

objects and colors can give you the feeling of having a new kitchen whenever you want it.

A Living Kitchen Is Never Done

The real beauty of design is that a living kitchen is never truly done. It changes in subtle ways, both in form and function. This means your kitchen is constantly evolving to become a place that mirrors who you are, and who you are becoming. So don't be afraid to make changes, whether it's replacing the curtains or changing where you keep the silverware. Your kitchen is made for living in. Allow your needs, desires, and passions to define the space, and it will always be the heart of your home.

And don't worry when that new-cabinet smell starts to wear off. If you've made good choices, your new kitchen will continue to enrich your life long after the work is done. Now that you have a brand-new kitchen, the journey is just beginning.

In fact, perhaps it's time to think about remodeling that bathroom . . .

Notes:

Notes:

Notes:

Notes: